PERFORMANCE

Delivering Your Own Awesome

Bruce Gandy

 FriesenPress

Suite 300 - 990 Fort St
Victoria, BC, V8V 3K2
Canada

www.friesenpress.com

Copyright © 2020 by Bruce Gandy
First Edition — 2020

Photo Credit Gary Brown.

ISBN
978-1-5255-6625-7 (Hardcover)
978-1-5255-6626-4 (Paperback)
978-1-5255-6627-1 (eBook)

1. MUSIC, INSTRUCTION & STUDY

Distributed to the trade by The Ingram Book Company

TABLE OF CONTENTS

FOREWORD

My friendship with Bruce Gandy goes back many years, closer to fifty than forty. Our close personal relationship was founded in, and grounded in, piping. As young boys and teenagers, we played pipes together in the City of Victoria Pipe Band, and we competed against one another as amateurs and professionals.

Outside the realm of piping we have shared many important life experiences: from Bruce's hole-in-one at Cedar Hill Golf Club, weddings, children, loss of parents, laughs, despair —we've shared it all. His Donald MacDonald Quaich, which he won in 2015, sits proudly on the bar in my home.

And through all of this, I've had a "front row seat" to the remarkable piping and piping career that is Bruce Gandy. There are many people who have talent of one type or another, but very few have a gift. Bruce falls into the latter. His extraordinary piping, as all of us who have heard him over the years know, is unique and remarkable.

So it may surprise people to learn that Bruce has, from the time he was a young boy, suffered from the same anxiousness and fears that many people experience when performing music. His gift does not relieve him of these feelings. Indeed, he suffered from this more than many pipers I know. Yet, he found a way to overcome this. In piping, our generation was taught to play, but not necessarily to perform.

Through his experiences, including both successes and struggles, Bruce has learned how to best prepare himself for the recital stage and competition platform. His greatest piping successes have come relatively later in his career, when he was able to thoughtfully address his competitive demons.

In these pages, Bruce offers practical and heartfelt advice and solutions that will help people maximize their performance, no matter what their craft. His "One-Eighty Factor" helps to change thinking and perspective, turning from negative thoughts to positive.

Bruce's genuine love of piping and teaching piping is evident in these pages. As well, it resides in his charitable foundation, and he lives and breathes it every day.

Peter Aumonier
October 2019

PREFACE

*The artist is nothing without the gift,
but the gift is nothing without the work*

—Emile Zola

Bruce in performance at Benaroya Hall, Seattle, 2016. Photo Credit Steve Baughn

A few years ago, I attended a conference and I got chatting with an author who, after much back and forth about our work, said to me, "If you have something to say, write a book. If you have a story to tell, well, that is even better!"

As a music coach who frequently travels to teach workshops, I found that many of my small reference note pages were getting more information and detail attached each time. Learning from other people's experiences on the mechanical, the physical, and, especially, the mental elements of performance has woken up my own vision to give me much more clarity into the subject.

When I first started to perform, as a much younger person, I was a very nervous young boy. I didn't want my family around to see me play as I was scared of the performance not being perfect. I put all that pressure on myself and I had no idea why. It had never dawned on me that these people were listening with total hopes of musical enjoyment. I see that happening all of the time when I am coaching and adjudicating, and I now try to speak to performers and parents at length about it. It most likely took until I was a parent myself to understand that while a person is performing in a competition, the parent, or coach, or friend is really trying to send out the most positive vibes possible.

So why a book? Is there not enough self-help out there already? What more could I possibly say? These are the questions of self-doubt that have gone through my head since the start of this project a couple of years ago. Having anxiety, there are many times in which I live in a world of panic, and I often confront an inability to bring projects to 100 percent completion. It's always easier to back away from something that is not quite finished than risk a less-than-perfect outcome. It is much easier to say, "I'll fix it later" or "I'll perform the next time an opportunity comes up". This book is a great personal challenge for me, because it relates to something so emotionally close to me.

I have coached thousands of people, in bands, private settings, workshops, and clinics, over the past thirty-five years. With that experience I believe I can safely say that the number one issue at almost all levels is self-doubt in one's own ability, combined with a fear of live performance.

I went from being a young person just learning an instrument, to getting involved with a local group, and very soon, by the time I was nine or ten years old, I was competing or doing local performances. On days of competitions, as much as I truly loved the playing part, I could not eat breakfast and did not want to talk to anyone about it. I didn't understand what was going on, even though I was still getting nice applause and encouragement from more experienced players, as well as winning some good prizes.

Fast forward ten years and I was performing many recitals in various parts of the world. I was now confident in my ability. And yet, while I usually had a set list with me, I still didn't have the ability or the know-how to engage the audience. I often thought, "It is difficult to figure out a crowd if you don't say anything at all to them."

Performances are still difficult, especially the beginning. But I have learned a great deal over the years on how to prepare for them. Nowadays, nothing excites me more than being in a room full of interested people and being able, with the mere tone of an instrument and the movement of fingers, to transform those people to a different place than the one they were in when they came into the venue. This is the end result—the positive aspect of this book and what this book means.

At times when I coach and listen, I get to hear some of my students accomplish this. They are well prepared, and they are focused, and all of the stars seem to align to make something magical happen. They are just "feeling it" and the playing comes out without effort. Even at a lower, less-than-technically-perfect level, they rise above on that day to perform at their own "World Best." They are not thinking hard or over-analyzing all. They are just doing it.

Many great athletes show this particular ability when it counts. Two very famous ones that have been studied for years are Michael Jordan and Wayne Gretzky. No one really knows how they do it. They just seem to see the whole court or rink, and some instinct tells them what to do. Gretzky just knew where the puck was going to be, and he put himself into position to act on it. I believe that some of that is partly instinctual, but also due to years of really working on the "watch and listen" compo-nent. So, on game day, it just happened.

When musicians are ready, prepared, and feel good about everything, that same inner greatness can occur.

I am not a trained writer and I do not bring you this book armed with hundreds of studies on musicians, athletes, and psychology. I was not trained at the university level to create different studies. However, I do come as an extremely passionate musician, performer, competitor, workshop leader, and coach. I have been very fortunate to sit in the same room as many other great coaches over time to learn firsthand. I have also been fortunate to have some big highlighted moments over time. These have allowed me to reflect on many of the topics listed in this book.

Not all of them are first place victories. Some are actually musical disasters, which you will read about later on. In fact, while reflecting back over the years, some of the biggest moments have come during (non-competition) recital performances.

A couple of evenings spring to mind right away. In 2015, I was invited to teach a group and perform in a town called Bad St. Leonhard in Austria (about three hours away from Vienna). There is a keen group of bagpipers in that area and there was a town festival planned in which they were to do a concert. They had asked if I and a fellow piper could each do a twenty-minute spot on the stage there. We both picked tunes that had stories attached to them and one of the band's people translated our stories to the crowd for us. What is most memorable is that we were two completely different cultures, one on that stage and the other the audience, and our connection was music. That connection was wonderful! Add to that the fact that we played in an acoustically beautiful church ruin that was over a thousand years old. It was a beautiful sunny August evening, perfect climate, and I came off stage wishing that I could have played for an hour. Several people came up and introduced themselves to both of us afterward to thank us and try in their very best English to tell us that this piping was a beautiful cultural experience for them. That night is something that will stay with me for a long time.

I grew up as a child in Victoria, British Columbia, going out each month to play at the Vancouver Island Pipers Club. We were encouraged to get up and perform at all levels. It was during my younger years there that I was able to watch some of the greatest players of the time perform. Often, the top pipers from Scotland would be over for a contest or seminar and would come to Victoria to perform. There are tunes and visuals still in my head some forty-plus years later and I remember them like they were yesterday. That is the impression that these great performers left on me, and I have strived to try to offer that same feeling to others.

Pipe Major E Raymond Gandy.

In 2002 I was very fortunate to win my first Highland Society of London Gold Medal at Inverness, Scotland. There are only two gold medals of this standard. The competitions are held annually, one at the Argyllshire Gathering in Oban, Scotland, and the other at the Northern Meeting in Inverness, Scotland. You can only win these medals once, so it is a very significant club to belong to. After that moment, there was a lot of wonderful press, and the group running the pipers club in Victoria asked if I would be interested in performing a recital for the evening during Easter week when I would be back out there visiting my family and friends.

In Victoria, the local papers, radio, and television were very responsive and gave some great press leading up to the event about the local boy coming back home to play from Dartmouth, Nova Scotia, where I have lived the past eighteen years.

I arrived and did an initial sound check (an acquaintance was going to be filming the performance) and then retired to a back room for a while to settle in and warm up myself and instrument.

When I came out to play, I was absolutely overwhelmed with the support. The place was packed. Hundreds were there in the room showing support. There were "older folks" whom I remembered from the days when I was a young kid. There were lots of young newer musicians doing what I used to do, sitting and listening with hopes of hearing something that they maybe play themselves. There was even a large group of non-musical folks, including neighbours from the street where I grew up as a young boy. That was magical all in itself, being back home where I grew up once again.

I had never seen that many people in that room, and on that night I didn't have a worry at all. It was easy to deliver that night. Music and energy poured out for the two fifty-five-minute sets. People were smiling, others had their eyes closed and just rocked back and forth. These people had come out and wanted a reason to feel good, and my playing on that night helped. I honestly cannot remember if I had technical errors. In fact, I am sure I did. But they were so unimportant that they are gone from memory.

Having the opportunity to talk to so many of them over snacks and refreshments later on really drove the message home: It wasn't about winning prizes or getting paid a fee for playing. I realized that all of the practices and rehearsals are so important to be able to put yourself in a place of confidence to deliver the music to the audience. And if you get to perform in front of a group that is genuinely happy for you, and you can channel that back through your music, then you "Deliver Your Own Awesome" and the feeling of joy will be with you forever. It is passion for the music. This passion is what it is all about for me. It's what I strive to deliver in my playing or coaching each day.

This was the real beginning to what propelled me to start a charity some ten years later to help build tuition scholarships to deserving pipers.

It is this passion that I hope to instill in you, the reader. I have spent my career pursuing it, and have learned many positive and negative aspects of performing. It is also something you can work on, to help deliver and improve each time you perform. And now I want to teach *you* how you can "Deliver Your Own Awesome." It isn't a miracle. This is something you can work on, to help deliver and improve each time you perform. In the remaining chapters we will explore various methods of practice and rehearsal, from journaling and recording to tapping into your inner fearless self, with the goal of bringing you to your very best through confident mastery of your own performance.

The rest of this book will lay out the various steps you can take to make this happen. I call it the Total Preparation Package (TPP).

This book is divided into three related sections: focusing on the technical (Learning Tunes), preparing for the event (Rehearsal), and delivering your own awesome (Performance). In each section I will lay out what my experience has taught me. For example, in Learning Tunes, we will look at how to practice with specific goals and how not to get overwhelmed. We will learn about the value of self-recording, and other tips. We will even discuss the importance of immersing yourself in every opportunity to listen and watch and learn from top performer and players.

In Rehearsal, we will talk about what it takes to make the most out of getting ready for an event: to practice with commitment, to find the love in what you do and use it to motivate you, and to look for ways to bring joy to your practice and develop confidence in yourself. We will also talk about the value of visualization and setting up opportunities to play in ways that make it feel like you are already there on performance day.

In "Performance," we will talk about all the ways you can help yourself get focused and ready to play "for real." Here is where I will introduce the "One-Eighty Factor," which helped me when I needed it most.

Finally, we will look at ways to keep the momentum going and complete the full circle. These are strategies that can help you grow—anything from learning how you can improve by teaching others, to gaining confidence by learning how to lead and inspire others.

All of these are my insights that I have learned from years of experience. And I want to share them with you, to help you "Deliver Your Own Awesome."

Word Art-The Positive Thoughts.

PART ONE
Learning Tunes

We are what we repeatedly do.
Excellence then, is not an act, but a habit.

—*Aristotle*

Romana Brunner receiving guidance, Austria, 2015. Photo Credit Christian Minibek

The first step in the Total Preparation Package (TPP) that will help you "Deliver Your Own Awesome" is an obvious one: learn your tunes.

Now, that sounds simple, but it is not. Many students figure that learning a tune is just rote repetition—playing a song through over and over again, maybe stopping where they don't do so well and running through that part a couple of times, but then moving on.

Repetition doesn't make you better. Repeating *excellence* makes you better.

To practice excellence repeatedly you have to learn how to focus, to prepare, to plan. By following the steps outlined here, you will make your practice more efficient and effective.

SECTION 1
Practice with Purpose

As you're working on a new piece of music or in a new area in your craft or sport, there are several stages in the Total Preparation Package (TPP) to bring you from zero (brand-new) to the actual performance area. The bookends of this process surrounding the many stages of practice and rehearsal that fall in the middle will be important, and you should identify with those as often as possible.

Using music for this central example, we may have a series of steps like this:

- **The main idea.** Here is a new piece that you get to hear, or perhaps you see the sheet music. This step is about *planting a seed of interest* in your mind. This starting point is where you store the idea or thought and get ready to face it head on.
  In any sport, this could possibly be the point where you see a coach implement some new fundamentals; for example, in your golf swing.
- **Emerge from idea to beginning steps of mastering the piece.** This is where you have your sheet music and perhaps a recording or video and *you begin to work through it.* Generally, there is a spectrum of approaches that are taken by the student at this stage.
- On the one hand, some might work very hard at playing the tune absolutely technically correct, but without any sense of feel for the song. For example, you might work through a piece at a slower pace or tempo than the music is usually performed at, playing all of the technical elements with good clarity. This may be your purpose, which is fine, but you need to remind yourself that just playing all of the black and white parts of the page correctly does

not mean that the piece is complete. In fact, it is far from complete. Analytical people often fall into this category.

- On the other hand, a student might pick up the piece and play it with great enjoyment and abandon, but with several technical elements missing. They may be in a hurry and have a good feel for music, as well as good sight-reading skills. They may be able to make the song flow at a recognizable pace. People with naturally smooth or quicker hands often fall into this category.

- Depending on how your mind works and the stage of development you are at, one of these traits will likely show through more strongly than others. Sometimes, depending on the person, *both* may be happening. The judging in figure skating used to be a great example of both of these disciplines. The skaters were marked first for the compulsory figures (the technical elements of the performance) and then for the artistic performance. One could not survive successfully without the other. Some skaters have amazing feet, showing strength and great discipline, while a different skater may have had previous dance or ballet training, or have natural ability, and they simply glide along the ice.

- Regardless of which you naturally gravitate to, you now have to focus your purpose on *bringing up the less natural side*. Here, the helpful coach is welcome. A coach will help identify your strengths and weakness and offer you good direction in how to improve the weaker, less comfortable areas. They can help you concentrate on those areas and give you a plan that gives you a purpose for your practicing.

- **Identify at the beginning of the work session what you will be trying to accomplish this day**. Spending a few minutes to think and plan out logically how you want to spend your valuable practice time can greatly increase the results. Be ready to practice as if you were showing up for a work assignment. You want to have all of your papers ready, if you need them. Make sure your maintenance tools are all at hand, right down to a sweat towel.

If you feel like you might record a part of the session, have that equipment all set up before you start.

- The whole idea of practicing with purpose is to get the most out of your time while you are actually working at your craft, whether it is music or a sport. If you can start to make progress and get into a "zone" then you do not want to waste five or ten minutes going out to your car to grab something that you have forgotten. You will lose focus and take time to get back to where you were.

- You may go through the piece up to tempo to discover, first, how much of the playing is coming through clearly, and second, to hear the phrases or embellishments that need attention to bring them up to that level. It is a good suggestion when you start implementing this plan to have a practice book or journal. This records the progress you are making and also serves to remind you of the "to do" areas.

- *When journaling any of your practice session, it is important to be honest with yourself on the progress as well as the work needed in particular areas.* It's very easy to say what is incorrect, but you must remind yourself of the progress that you are making as you go. Many small steps in each session will add up to good progress before too long.

I personally use journaling for all of the above. When I am preparing for a concert, I am playing a lot more than just one piece and I may not be able to cover it all in a practice session. Having a dedicated area to write this down helps to keep you on top of your progress and perhaps time spent on different elements for the upcoming event. When you actually look at your journal, you can see that perhaps you have not worked on song X or have not checked on the maintenance of the instrument in a while. Writing these items down reminds you to do this next time and strengthens the commitment to actually doing it. I personally journal as I close in on an event to help remind me of what needs tidying up, and while I think as an experienced performer I will remember all of the different bits of music, I found that I often "favoured" some music compared to less time on others.

When I am coaching and we are trying to progress through a certain piece, I like to journal here as well. It's amazing how good the progress becomes when I have asked students to mark down notes on all three aspects of our performance expectations: tonal, musical, and technical. A metronome can become very handy to a person as a reference when they know, for example, that Tune A played at forty-eight beats per minute was quite well-executed and phrased but lacked much musical definition. Playing the same tune at sixty-eight was much nicer musically and had lots of lift and energy to it, but most likely unclear handwork. So, we use those numbers to try to find the balance between accurate and musical, and the metronome marking can give you a solid hint as to how well you do, at what tempo.

You may have noticed how many people keep a scorecard (journal) when they go to the gym. It may tell of amount of reps, or the weight on a particular machine, or the speed and incline settings of their treadmill. This gives you a starting point, and you can journal the process and your results.

You can use the journal however you like, but I recommend using it so you see what you've worked on, the progress, and notes for improvements. Trying to remember all of that after a practice session, whether it is music or sport, is very difficult.

Remember that journaling does not have to just be a book. Part of journaling could be documenting items on video so you can look back, and even making a video note yourself. Writing down what you felt from a recording may come out very black and white on paper but if you filmed the recording, you can come back and perhaps re-watch when you're trying to understand exactly what your written note means. With some training you will be able to identify both the good areas and the less than perfect areas. You and your coach can then plan which exercises would be of best use at that point to strengthen your current piece.

Eliminate many potential issues with the use of a recorder. It is often difficult to perform nicely and musically without having control of all of the technical elements. *Listening back to a recording of yourself* will help you identify both the good areas and the less than perfect areas. This in turn will help you to identify which exercises would be of best use to strengthen your current piece.

Your purpose here is to listen or watch back and become a bit of your own coach, no matter what level you are at. Your purpose is *not* to be able to identify all of the incorrect elements only, but within that, you must be able to identify the "why." This will help lead you down the new path of repairing what you feel is incorrect. It's often very easy to say that something is incorrect, but that serves no purpose in my mind to help you. If you are judging or scoring an event, then sure, identify what is incorrect. But as a practice tool, you must have an idea of how to solve that issue if you are to improve.

I coach so many people that might tell me about how their performance went at an event: "I was doing okay, but then I did this and then that and then I screwed up final part." They feel that if they identify and know the slips, then magically they won't do them next time and all will be fine. But you want the ability to either understand the fault and how to fix, or have your personal coach point out what is incorrect (but not always in a negative way, which can lead to a big lack of confidence). As a coach, or even as you listen or watch back yourself, the purpose of this exercise should be to point out why the element is perhaps not as strong as the other parts. So instead of thinking of it as a negative, or a minus, try to show why it's just not "as good as" other parts.

A typical example for me after a weekend competition as a coach could be something like this: One student may say, "It was awful. I missed this and that, and player B sounded great. I didn't have a chance." A second players might say, "I felt I played really well today. I felt good, quite relaxed, and if I didn't have those little slips, I think I could have been way up in the list. I just need to make sure I get enough warm up first and take that deep breath before starting, so I don't speed up and get myself into trouble. This was an easy thing to fix and it's disappointing, but I know that those things are just mechanics."

Beautiful pond, or mental distraction?

The first player has not even thought about any decent part of the whole performance, and it's tough to build on that, whereas the second person understands that it's not "awful"; we just need to isolate certain areas and then try to improve in those areas. This exact same scenario I've seen and been guilty of myself on the golf course.

It can be good to add seriousness into your practice session. Get yourself ready as if it was the live performance. That includes having a drink ready, a towel, and the recording machine up and on standby.

Pick a random time to perform. If you started practice at 7 p.m. at night, tell yourself you are on at, say, 7:38 p.m.

Warm up, work on the tuning of your instrument, and go through one or many of your tunes or routines—whatever you like to do—as if you were to get ready to perform. You can play over your performance piece five times if you really want to but . . .

Once it's 7:38, you stop a moment and, pretending like the organizer just sent you up to the stage to play, you may even walk out of your room and back in. Think about that minute where you would be addressing the judge. If it helps, say hello to the judge or the audience. Of course, you are pretending, as no one is watching. And if they are, even better. Greet them, be confident, introduce the piece you are playing, and then turn on the machine (if you haven't already done so).

Take a minute or two, if needed, to set up the instrument and relax your nerves. Retune, if necessary. *Try to tune your pipes if needed!* Don't tell me you can't do it! Try. You certainly won't learn it if you don't at least move a drone.

After that, get ready, relax, play a few tuning phrases, then take a big deep breath and start. Don't just blow up your pipes and go. There is no control in that, and it *looks* like there is no control.

Most important is to make this exercise as close to a real competition or the recital stage. You only get one try. If it doesn't work, great, that's okay. You can plan to do it again. The more you get into the visualization of it all, the better you will become at the process, and the next live event will seem like nothing, as you have done it in your mind several times.

There is no point in making four recordings and using the best one. You need to train to be ready to play that *one*.

People's abilities will always vary greatly in either music, dance, or sport. Practicing with purpose may have many more stages for some than this section relates. Or it may be combined into fewer steps, depending on how you work things through between yourself and your coach. What is most important with this initial step is that you have a *proper purpose* to your practice. This will help speed up the learning process and produce a much higher level of accuracy and fluidity as you move into the rehearsal and performance phases.

KEY TAKEAWAYS

❖ PRACTICE WITH PURPOSE TO ARRIVE AT YOUR GOALS SOONER.

❖ IDENTIFY WHAT YOU ARE AIMING TO ACCOMPLISH.

❖ JOURNALING FOR PROGRESS—KEEP TRACK OF HOW FAR YOU'VE COME.

❖ JOURNALING FAULTS IS EASY; REMIND YOURSELF OF THE SMALL STEPS OF PROGRESS.

Your Personal Notes and Experiences

- What are your own reminders from this chapter?

....

....

....

....

....

....

....

....

....

....

....

....

....

....

....

....

....

....

For more information visit www.brucegandymusic.com

Small Steps, But Aim Big

Whether you think you can, or you think you can't—you're right.
—Henry Ford

This is a familiar saying for many people, but which one are you? As kids just starting out at our craft, it's quite easy to envision and think big. The imagination of young people is vibrant. As I coach students from teenagers to young adults to older adults, I notice that the more real-life experience one has, the harder it is for them to "aim BIG." As people age, many people have demanding jobs, grinding it out all day with little time to think of the "what if" scenario. They sink into the reality of the day-to-day grind that will not allow them to "aim big" and this can affect their after-hours pursuits, be it sport or music.

There are many exceptions to the rule though. Not only do many musicians and athletes find a way to "aim big," our society is in a wonderful state of change right now due to the minds of those who refuse to let the status quo run their lives. Entrepreneurial think tanks and seminars are popping up everywhere. Business people go to these and often spend a great part of the day playing games of all sorts. Some of these are children's games like water balloon fights, running with an egg on a spoon, or other fun games. The goal of these activities is to take this business person or entrepreneur back to their child's state of mind, where everything is fun and safe and it's okay to just do it, have a laugh, and dream big for your company.

As children play, I still hear them yelling, "Okay, next goal wins the cup!" The score might be seven goals to one already, but when this final challenge is issued, these kids are able to envision themselves playing on the big field or big arena, like their idols, and rise to the occasion.

The same process happens with music. Great rock and roll movies have been made around this. You would probably have a hard time finding friends who have not tried to be the great air guitar player at a rock concert. They stand there, acting it out as if they have the guitar in hand. Perhaps they are emulating a famous drummer, piano player, or even horn player to that effect. This is an important part of just letting go and letting the big dream work.

Many people have a fear of failure or embarrassment at times and will not admit to it publicly, but most of us have also tried some form of acting out the big dream.

Dreaming or aiming big is an envisioning tool that helps you to see what the end result can be. It doesn't always work the first time to help you hit greatness in your craft, but used as a positive force enough times, you soon begin to ask yourself, "Why can't I do that?"

With young children we let them play and just go for it. But as adults this is much tougher to execute, as many adults see the risks and the negative side of what's wrong or what can go wrong.

So, while you are trying to aim big, you also need to use the "how to" part of your mind and map out a plan. This is not to discourage you and force you into the small, labour-intensive work plan and forget about the dream. Rather, use the dreamed-of result as a plan of steps that help you see how to reach your own personal goal.

Years of personal study interviewing other musicians and athletes have taught me that writing down your goals on paper and then working on an action plan to reach them greatly increases your chance of success. Depending on your goal, you may have yearly brackets, monthly, weekly, or even daily goals. The smaller and more refined the step is, the easier it is to accomplish.

- Write down the goal. (Example: write a book.)
- Think hard about a manageable size. (Write a chapter or edit part of it.)
- Downsize to reality. (Set aside thirty minutes a day to write.)

- Reward that small task with a check mark—you have to see some form of progress to keep continuing!

Keeping these steps small helps to continue moving forward. Dream big and keep a record of the little successes as you go so you can track the progress and see how far you have gone along that road.

Writing this chapter, I'm reminded of a quote that has always been with me. I grew up in a small house with many brothers and sisters around and we had to share rooms, often two and sometimes three to a room. My middle brother of three older brothers was a big believer in the words of John F. Kennedy. In 1963 he quoted George Bernard Shaw speaking to the Irish Parliament. In our room was an 8 x 11, cream-coloured sheet of paper in a simple black frame with the quote: "Some men see things as they are and say why, I dream things that never were and say why not." I used to read that every day in our room at seven or eight years old and was never sure if I understood it for many years, but I never forgot it.

Dream big! Dream of the "why nots." If you find a reason that you cannot do something, write it down and dream of ways to fix it!

KEY TAKEAWAYS

- ❖ PRACTICE MORE THAN NORMAL.

- ❖ ENGRAIN THE PROCESS INTO YOUR HEAD WITH MORE TIME SPENT PRACTICING.

- ❖ KEEP LEARNING.

- ❖ TAKE SMALL STEPS, BUT AIM BIG.

- ❖ DREAM BIG ENOUGH TO ENVISION THE END GOAL.

- ❖ KEEP TRACK.

- ❖ WRITE GOALS DOWN ON PAPER. DREAM IT, BELIEVE IT, BE IT.

- ❖ BE ACCOUNTABLE TO YOURSELF.

- ❖ BUILD A STEP BY STEP ACTION PLAN TO SUCCEED.

Your Personal Notes and Experiences

- What are your own reminders from this chapter?

....

....

....

....

....

....

....

....

....

....

....

....

....

....

....

....

....

....

....

....

For more information visit www.brucegandymusic.com

SECTION 3
Get the Most Out of Your Time

To get the best results from your practice schedule, analyze your current routine and make the necessary changes to make your practice time more efficient. So, what might these changes be?

Focus first on what you need to accomplish in the session most and then lay out a plan that is efficient while allowing you to enjoy your time. An obvious and common scenario is the student who spends an hour or so just playing through music one tune after another. Then, when the time is up, he calls it a day. Although in most cases this is an inefficient use of practice time, there are occasions when this type of practice may be used. For example, a student might need repetitions over a single piece to bring it to a state where it can be refined, or at least partially memorized. Or, as a bagpiper, you may be blowing in a new and stiff reed, so concentrating on the fine points in a tune is impossible. These types of sessions I call *logging time*. Remember, even when you are logging time, you can still improve on the important area of stamina that a good performance requires.

Let's go back to basics and examine the benefits of good practicing. A good solid performance consists of the three basic fundamentals of playing: *tone*, *technical work*, and most important, *music*. When you hear an excellent performance by a top performer in competition or recital, you should notice a combination of all three of these fundamentals.

Although *tone* is very important, we won't go into the fine points here, as it warrants a whole separate chapter. I mention it here as a reminder to ensure that players check over their instruments for proper maintenance each time they play! Basic mechanical maintenance, like proper checks for leaks, accounts for approximately 80–90 percent of the problems experienced by young pipers with an inefficient instrument. Get into the habit of checking your instrument and tuning it each time you play—at the beginning, middle, and end of the practice session; you will greatly increase your awareness of the instrument and your ability to control it.

The *technical work* on melody, embellishments, and particularly how the embellishments affect the melody, is often overlooked by many players. When you have a technical problem in a tune, it's wise to ask yourself why the problem is occurring. An inexperienced player may have a problem simply because she is unskilled in some form of playing—e.g., any technical movement required for their piece. In this case, the problem is easily addressed by working or developing your own form of a scale exercise containing the problem movement. This will be much more efficient than playing the entire tune over and over and getting upset because of one recurring slip.

If most of the basic exercises have been learned and worked on, you may find that you have to take matters a step further by troubleshooting a particular area of a tune. Quite often, due to repetition of a tune, one little area is troublesome and requires extra work; for any number of reasons, it's just not flowing. By breaking down the embellishment, or playing only the bars before and after the problem, you may be able to discover the real problem more quickly.

When breaking down the movement or bar of music, ask yourself these questions when analyzing the piece:

- Is the technical movement or embellishment being played correctly?
- Is the timing/rhythm of that area of the tune being played correctly?
- Do you understand the theory behind what you are playing?
- Is the technical movement embellishing or adding colour to the music?

Often, the last two questions will help you understand the theoretical and rhythmical aspects of playing in different time signatures, most notably the difference between 2/4 and 6/8 time. By spending a minute to carefully assess the rhythmic structure of a tune, you can gain insight into how the tune should sound. Understanding how a technical embellishment is either helping or disturbing the flow of a tune can save hours of frustrating work later on.

Two of the best tools for practicing are a *metronome* and an *audio recorder*. A metronome can feel strange at first, but gradually you will get used to playing along with it. Many people who do not like a metronome are precisely those who could benefit the most from it. In piping, I would venture to say that playing in absolutely perfect time is not a necessity—especially as a soloist—but keeping close to the target number of beats per minute (bpm) is important. For those who pipe for highland dancing or play with the accompaniment of other musicians, it is good to have in your head a very firm idea of what 60 or 80 bpm is. Practicing with a metronome will help you to get there.

By far the most important practice tool is the audio recorder. A recording does not lie (assuming that the machine is in good working order and produces a reasonable quality). That's why I mentioned doing it in the "Practice with a Purpose" section. Piping is physical work, and since your heart is beating faster than normal, your judgement is not always as clear as you may think, particularly concerning tempo. Many times I have seen a player come off the contest stage thinking that they had played a nice smooth tune only to find out on the recording that it was much faster than they had felt up there.

This same miscalculation also occurs in tournament golf. As adrenaline rises, the player tends to hit the ball farther and must add that into their calculation when hitting their shots. When you can accept that nerves and adrenaline are affecting some part of your performance, you can then harness that power to help you elevate your own performance to an exciting new level.

So, now that you have made your recording, you need to spend some time *listening to it and learning from it.* But there is a right way and a wrong way to do this.

A recording allows you to sit down hours or days later to analyze your performance with a clear, undisturbed listen/view. Not only will a recording help you to define the areas of concern that need to be addressed, but it also *demonstrates the good aspects of your playing*. The wrong way is to approach it negatively. It is really easy to point out all the "bad" parts. Remember: You are your own worst critic. A recording tends to emphasize your faults. You must remember that when you go back to a recording and evaluate a performance, you should not be too hard on yourself; try to find a balancing mix of the good aspects in the performance as well. It is important that in reviewing a recording, you first *consider what you did well and create a positive thought pattern.* If you can recognize where you have done things well, you are halfway there and can strive to make the rest of the performance as good as those areas. Then, go on to critique what you did and identify areas that need adjustment.

Let's put these thoughts into a check list of things to remember when using an audio recorder:

- Was the rhythm correct?
- Does the tune have a musical feel?
- Was the tempo appropriate and steady?
- Was the playing crisp or clumsy?
- Were there any mistakes that you did not realize before?
- Isolate specific areas to improve on. Remember, you can't fix everything at once so don't even try. Practice as if your teacher is present, and build stamina training into your practice.
- Now let's step further back and consider setting goals for each practice session:
- Is the instrument tuned and working well? If not, too much time will be spent fighting the instrument and you won't be able to concentrate on playing music or the technical aspects of the piece.
- Are you practicing enough that physical conditioning doesn't interfere with your ability to concentrate on technique and melody?
- What technical areas need special attention?

- Understand the timing; review the difference between compound time vs. simple time.
- Use repetition to develop consistency.
  Use the audio recorder; it's your teacher's ears and enables you to plan and analyze your own practice. Find troublesome areas in the tune; isolate and emphasize them. Develop exercises for particular problems (e.g., any technical embellishment that is causing the flow of the tune to change). For example:
- Does your own playing sound melodic or mushy?
- Is the tune memorized accurately and thoroughly? This is critical to bring you to the rehearsal stage. If you do not know the piece accurately, you will spend time concentrating on what note to play rather than how to properly execute it.
- Are you playing at the correct speed/tempo/pace? Use your recorder. Time yourself. Use a metronome if necessary. Practice often under performance conditions to help train your internal clock.
- Without rhythm, where is the music? Does your own rhythmical interpretation fit the style of the tune? Does the rhythm flow smoothly or is the tempo uneven?
- Does the melody come from your heart or does it sound digital or computer generated.
- Is there good emotion and feel in the piece or is it clumsy and staccato?

The way that you think you play and the way that it comes out are often very different. Consult your recorder and become the teacher during the time between lessons. Later, your teacher's ears will help you to evaluate your playing. Your teacher's instruction will help to guide you toward your desired musical result. But in the meantime, your recorder can help you become your own teacher.

When you are confident in the way you are delivering the piece, your personal performance level will also rise.

KEY TAKEAWAYS

❖ USE YOUR TIME WISELY. WHAT ARE YOUR ESSENTIAL ELEMENTS OF STRENGTH AND WEAKNESS? FIND BOTH FOR OPTIMAL TIME USE.

❖ RECORD YOURSELF OFTEN TO REVEAL BOTH SUCCESSES AND FAULTS.

❖ PRACTICE ALL THE TIME AS IF YOUR COACH IS THERE WITH YOU.

❖ KEEP UP, PHYSICALLY. ARE YOU MAINTAINING A PLAYING STAMINA GOOD ENOUGH TO ENHANCE YOUR PERFORMANCE?

Your Personal Notes and Experiences

• What are your own reminders from this chapter?

....

....

....

....

....

....

....

....

....

....

....

....

....

....

....

....

....

....

....

For more information visit www.brucegandymusic.com

SECTION 4
Practice More Than Normal

The time that you spend on your craft, whatever it may be, is most directly tied to a competition or your upcoming game or live performance and is generally referred to as practice time. This is all the minutes, hours, days and weeks that you work at your craft to achieve a certain goal.

There are many forms of practice used in every discipline and they do not have to all be labour intensive for you to achieve "greatness" or "best in class." Greatness comes from a process of learning your craft first, whether this is piping, singing, acting, or gaming. You then add to this a solid amount of rehearsal time, which will take you up to the performance of your lifetime. Finally, you then follow up and move forward to begin the full circle once again.

But what does it mean to say *"practice more than normal"*? Is there a universal time on a clock quoting a certain allotment of minutes each day that adds up to "normal"? Well, of course not, as this would differ for almost everyone. *When people are taking on a new sport or instrument, there are usually a set of guidelines and expectations set by a coach dictating what normal actually is.* In music, that could be practicing alone for twenty minutes per day when you do not have your lesson or band practice, and in sport it could mean stretching or running each day before the team actually practices.

The word "normal" is not a definitive term for an activity. The dictionary definition of "normal" is really a list of descriptive words. One of these will perhaps trigger a thought: average, accustomed, acknowledged, commonplace, conventional, customary, general, habitual, mean, median, natural, orderly, ordinary, popular, prevalent, regular, routine, standard, traditional, typical and finally, unexceptional.

Once we start to think of what those words mean to us, we can have a gauge on what normal is and how to exceed it. Everything in life that we try to accomplish that is not part of our "normal" routine requires us to exceed the amount of work we would usually put in. Some objectives are easy and obvious to point to. For instance, walking or running more than usual for better heart health, or eating less food or better food while dieting. These are two simple examples of doing more than what was commonplace in an effort to lead yourself towards greater personal accomplishment.

Practicing more at your craft simply means that you put in more time than your usual amount or what the average team member is doing. This helps you to achieve your goals much more quickly, exceed your target, and feel good about your progress as the end result becomes much clearer.

Practicing is the basic learning of the music you will play, the adjustment to your baseball stance, or golf swing, or perhaps the change in your stride if you are a runner or skater, for instance. A variety of the skills are needed that we may call the mechanics of your discipline.

When you break down what it takes to reach personal greatness or an awesome performance, it all starts with learning the basics of the discipline and engraining the process into your head. You cannot do it in a day, but if you work at it carefully and *practice more than normal,* it stands to reason that you will arrive at your goal much sooner.

When you see biographies of great athletes, or musicians, who make it right to the top, you will almost always find that they were the people that stayed after the group or team practice and worked at their part longer. A love for the discipline develops and the more results you get, the more you want, so you work at it harder.

You must remember at times to take a break as well and take stock of where you are on your quest. Often, parents have to make their children come out of the pool, the court, or the rink just to rest them, so the kids can recharge for the next day. As adults, you tend to see that little bright light that you're chasing and want to get there now, but you need to just sit back at times and *mark the progress* and what goals you hit before moving onward to the next step.

KEY TAKEAWAYS

- ❖ ASSESS WHAT IS "NORMAL" AMONG YOUR TEAMMATES, BANDMATES, YOURSELF. GO THE "EXTRA MILE."

- ❖ FOCUS ON THE BASICS.

- ❖ LEARN TO LOVE THE DISCIPLINE OF PRACTICE.

- ❖ TAKE STOCK, DON'T EXPECT MIRACLES——BE IN IT FOR THE "LONG HAUL."

Your Personal Notes and Experiences

- What are your own reminders from this chapter?

....

....

....

....

....

....

....

....

....

....

....

....

....

....

....

....

....

....

....

For more information visit www.brucegandymusic.com

Listen/Watch

Excellence is doing ordinary things extraordinarily well.
—E. F. Schumacher

One of the most primitive and natural elements of practice for artists and athletes is the Listen/Watch method. You often hear and see sons and daughters of prominent artists becoming "good, or proficient" more quickly than others seem to. Other people justify their own lower level by saying things like "it's in their blood" or "they're destined to be great, just look at their parents."

There may be a hint of truth in that sentiment, but I believe the better explanation is the fact that the younger person has been immersed in that activity since infancy. I know that in my own house there were bagpipes going from the first days I can remember. And we had them in the house all the time while my son was growing up. While I have not spoken to him personally, I would be willing to be bet that Jack Nicklaus always made sure there were a few golf clubs and putters lying around for his sons Gary and Jack Jr. to play with. The advantage that these children and I received was the ability to just "play around" with it. Having someone near to answer questions all of the time, and/or having the equipment available to use, could be what gives a certain musician or athlete an advantage over others. A big part of being immersed into the activity is that all of the listening and watching gives you a certain familiarity before you actually become a player.

Now, instead of bemoaning the fact that you are at a disadvantage because the other player/band/team has all of these extra advantages and opportunities to Listen/Watch, try to put your energy into a "how do I close the gap" approach. Use your imagination. Figure out ways to adapt to situations that you will face. *Imagine yourself in that not-so-perfect situation, see yourself having a world-best finish after, and figure out how you got there.* There *is* a route. It's not all black and white, but there is a route. *And* you have to believe in yourself, most of all!

It all comes down to hard work and a will to succeed. Some people are quite happy to play at a certain level and do not want to constantly work hard to be the very best they can. If you are a casual runner, then this would be just fine. You may not win a race, but you're covering a distance much faster than just walking, and the other benefits of exercise outweigh the need to win.

However, in the music business, and especially in the bagpipe world, there are not many things that sound more unpleasant than listening to someone playing very poorly on an out-of-tune instrument. So, the need to *listen and watch* better performers is important in order to get yourself to that level, even just to be accepted in public.

When you see shows about team sports or music ensemble competitions, you often find that group watching the performance later on. This helps them to gain a better understanding of the performance, both good and not so good. Sure, it can be exciting to watch yourself on television or computer screen, but you can also use this viewing to see where improvement can be made.

As I mentioned in the previous section, it's very important when listening back to yourself or watching your routine that you don't just criticize what is wrong. You must strike a balance between quality critique and putting yourself down too much. *Instead of pointing out what is "wrong," ask yourself why it is "not as good" as other parts.* By doing that you are in the positive mind set of what it could or should be. Your thinking turns to how to play a passage correctly, or with more vigor or emotion. Or, in sport, perhaps think of how you could have made that play in the defensive zone better by observing your surroundings on the screen. This is much more positive than just saying that was incorrect and that's why I lost a point.

Listen/Watch. Most of you have done things like this in life, and when something doesn't go as planned it's much easier to just say why it was wrong, as opposed to pointing out *how to make it better.*

Practice can be very hard work, both physically and mentally. You may find that you do not have enough time in a day to work on the pieces that you are trying to master. Those lacking the determination, the drive, and the will to succeed use this as an excuse, whereas winners will find a way around this.

One of my adult bagpipe students, a mother of two young children and owner of a professional practice in town, is busy. But she also loves playing her pipes. She played for years as a young girl and then stopped for many years. She is very good, but determined to be much better, both as a performer and in competition. At a lesson, I made recordings of seven of her pieces that she is working on this season. She is not the fastest person at memorizing the music, so she needs more time at it. Finding quiet personal time as a mother of two and running a business is tough, but she was able to load all of the recordings onto her phone, which she then plays while driving back and forth to work.

This is a great use of her time and she will hear, for example, the first tune perhaps six or eight times, internalizing it before she attempts it on her own. How many of your friends can just sing a song from the radio because they have heard it enough? But now think of this: if you just gave them a lyric sheet and played the soundtrack, would they be able to sing it as well? It would be quite rare for this to happen. This is what the Listen/Watch method will do. It helps you to internalize the music, or that defensive play, so when you *do* physically attempt the activity, you have played it or watched it over and over in your head so much that you already feel that you know it.

This is really the biggest advantage that those young people have who are supposedly "born with it." I have heard my son play music in the house that he has never seen the score for. He tells me he really liked this tune and was going to compete with it, and he realized that he already knew the score from hearing me play it so often at home.

You can call that an advantage, which I would say it is, and feel sorry for yourself. Or you can think of the down-time that you have in any given day and put this method to use. Everyone is busy these days, so you must be creative. Some potential free time may come as you commute to work, or in the morning while taking a shower, or even while going for walks, or during those few minutes at night before bed.

In the end, using the Listen/Watch method as part of your practice routine can only help if you stay positive and stick with it. You'll wake up one day, much sooner than expected, thinking, "I already know that piece and I have not put much physical time into it at all!"

Then, the practicing will start to turn into real playing and rehearsing.

KEY TAKEAWAYS

❖ "DO WHAT I HEAR, PLAY AS I SEE!"

❖ LISTEN/WATCH THE VERY BEST PERFORMERS THAT YOU CAN.

❖ BRING A CONSTRUCTIVE AND POSITIVE APPROACH TO YOUR OWN RECORDINGS AND ASSESSMENTS.

❖ BE DETERMINED AND FIND OPPORTUNITIES TO LISTEN/WATCH WHENEVER YOU CAN.

Your Personal Notes and Experiences

- What are your own reminders from this chapter?

....

....

....

....

....

....

....

....

....

....

....

....

....

....

....

....

....

....

....

For more information visit www.brucegandymusic.com

PART TWO
Rehearsal

Bruce and Alex rehearse before The World Pipe Band Championships performance.

In preparing to "Deliver Your Own Awesome," practicing your fundamentals and technique is just the beginning. We all need to develop and maintain a rock-solid foundation; whether it is embellishments for piping or a good stance and swing for golf, without the basics we cannot hope to perform to our highest potential.

The *next* step in the Total Preparation Package (TPP) is one that very few people think: rehearsal practice. This is another whole combination of skill sets and routines that help you prepare for all the distractions and anxieties you might encounter when it comes time to perform in front of other people (whether they are family and friends in the audience at a recital, your friends on the links during a game, or judges at a competition). We often just assume that if we practice technique and play our tunes over and over again until we get better at them, we will just "magically" be able to play them in front of others. And when we find we haven't done this, when we get up and are nervous and distracted and don't play to our fullest potential, we are left puzzled and wondering why we failed and think it must be because we didn't practice *enough.*

What is actually true is that we did not practice enough of the right things. We need to learn to practice performance. We need to rehearse.

The next section will help you learn how to rehearse. It includes a set of techniques and ideas that can help you get ready to play in front of other people, such as how to concentrate in the face of distraction, how to grow more confident in your playing, and how to stay committed and find the fun and enjoyment of performing. We also talk about how to stay motivated.

In the end, you will learn what you need to do to get ready for your next competition or performance, so that when you step up to play, you have already experienced and prepared for most of the distractions and things you will encounter.

Practice with Commitment

It takes willpower to switch off the world, even for an hour. It can feel uncomfortable and can upset some people. But it's better to disappoint a few people over small things than surrender your practice and focus to an empty inbox.

—Mark McGuinness

Some days we have fun days in our music or sport. This can be socializing with friends for a game of pickup, or just "jamming" to some new songs/tunes. These are important days to keep the fun and interest in your craft. However, to be awesome, world class, or at least perform to your very best potential, you have to sit down most days and practice with commitment, concentration, and focus.

Commitment to your music or sport means that you will attempt to consistently dedicate a certain amount of time daily, to work on the technical, physical, mental, and musical elements of your craft, so you can achieve the performance goals that have been set out for you.

You cannot just "play" at it. This can cause so much more work in the end with all the back tracking you end up doing.

Here's an example that I use myself when teaching others about concentration and focus. When I belonged to a gym to work out, before I started working out at home, I had a routine to follow involving warm up, the circuit, cardio work, then stretching. The warm up was easy as it was exactly that, warming up the body and getting good blood flow. The stretching at the finish was also not too challenging as it was a routine to follow. (Making sure I saved enough time to stretch out was the main challenge.)

Doing the circuit with the different machines and the cardio section was where I needed to concentrate and focus, so I could continue to progress there. As I would start to get used to machines, I would add more weight and repetitions here, but occasionally I would be sore, and not the good kind of workout aches. This was due to me trying to achieve numbers or reps, but not executing correctly, which is what often happens in music. Much like a recording device, the gym had two sources of help for me. The machines gave me weights and numbers, so I could track the routine, but more importantly, the gym has mirrors and trainers. Very often I would have to take an exercise and end it in front of the mirror with a slightly lower weight or stretch to ensure my posture was okay and I was not hurting myself. This would allow me to continue to move forward in training.

These mirrors acted much the same as an audio or video recorder does. You can work on a particular movement, but when you turn on the recording device, you have to concentrate and focus with great intensity to ensure you are executing correctly.

Is your posture correct? Are you sitting or standing up correctly with your instrument? As a coach, I often find that when a student corrects a particular spot in any piece they are playing, they just want to play it quicker and quicker six or eight times over. But they miss a few times, which shows that they are not concentrating and focusing. This is when the performer becomes very good at doing something incorrectly, and now the element or phrase becomes even more difficult to fix. Slow things down, focus really hard and execute the movement or part correctly seven, eight, or even ten times. Then, later on, you can slightly increase the pace.

Make sure you are not only recording to help review this yourself, but that you have a personal coach and make use of this coach as often as possible to review. I am fifty-seven years old at the time of writing, and I still record myself often and send the recordings along to my mentors and some peers to get feedback, positive or negative, so I can continue to grow.

One area that I got into some years back, and actually heard one of my peers talk about in a workshop session, was what is called *Practicing*

Concentration. Depending on what type of music or sport you play, there are varying levels of distraction which you may or may not face when performing. As a bagpipe coach and performer/competitor, I can tell you first-hand that some of the major difficulties to delivering your own awesome performance are the endless forms of distraction that we encounter at highland games or any event. Most of the people that I coach are used to that room in their house, alone, where they focus in on what they are playing. Then, while they feel they are well rehearsed and ready to perform, they now have to do it with all of these new distractions.

Here are a few of the things we deal with, in comparison to working on our own at home:

- Many people watching, which puts pressure on the performer.
- Vehicles driving in and out of the parks, sometimes very close.
- Families running around the area with kids who are playing, having fun, and being noisy, (which, by the way, they should be doing).
- Big loud power generators, which create a tonal nightmare when trying to tune the instruments.
- People wanting to talk to you at a time when you need to focus on getting ready to perform.
- Sheepdog or other animal displays in action and close to your performing platform.
- Loud, full pipe bands warming up close to you.
- Uncomfortable weather (hot or too cold), affecting ability to move your fingers well.

These are just a few of the distractions the musician may face at a public venue when performing. We need to learn how to face these head on and be able to maintain an ability to focus.

The term *Practicing Concentration* is a term I incorporate into my personal rehearsal time, as well as when I am coaching. Starting on my own, I will sometimes put on music, or, more often, turn the television on to create a distraction. I keep it in my view yet try to maintain focus on what I am working on. Other times I will plug in the dehumidifier so that I can try to think around the sound of the motor. I work on that, and then try to envision myself performing at a noisy outdoor venue. This helps me to prepare for those real situations.

Often when I am coaching I will tell the student that I am going to be distracting them and we work on overcoming this. I may get up and walk around, close to them, or just stretch my arms out. Perhaps make some noises. I have even resorted to throwing little paper balls at them. Of course, I don't physically harm the person, but I do try to bring an annoying level of distraction so the student can really try to practice their concentration and focus.

In the end, when the player arrives at the venue, which is completely different from their usual rehearsal space, they can start to answer all of those "what do I do if?" questions. Instead of complaining and worrying, they can use these new skills and eliminate some or most of the issues.

Understanding your potential distractions will definitely help you to also overcome some of the performance anxiety issues you may be facing. Remember that practicing with commitment is not only about doing it every day right after dinner, for example. Daily repetition of a task is *part* of what forms the habit. Commitment is about the *time*, the *effort*, the *concentration* and *focus*. Apply these to your routine and your positive rehearsals will lead you to awesome performance.

KEY TAKEAWAYS

❖ COMMIT TO A SPECIFIC TIME AND LENGTH OF PRACTICE.

❖ RECORD YOURSELF IN ORDER TO FOCUS AND CONCENTRATE.

❖ CREATE DISTRACTIONS AND LEARN HOW TO AVOID THEM OR IGNORE THEM.

❖ FOLLOW YOUR PRESCRIBED ROUTINE WHEN REHEARSING.

Your Personal Notes and Experiences

- What are your own reminders from this chapter?

....

....

....

....

....

....

....

....

....

....

....

....

....

....

....

....

....

....

For more information visit www.brucegandymusic.com

SECTION 2
Love What You Do

"Love what you do" could be listed under any of the main chapters in this book, but I chose the middle tier of rehearsal for this heading, as it helps to strengthen the difference between ordinary practice and performance rehearsal. Whether it is music, sport, or public speaking, you choose your topic often because you like/love the idea. That feeling alone can get you to start and move through the working parts on a project.

Through my teaching and clinics, I speak to many people throughout the year on a huge variety of topics surrounding the music I play. I do love the aspect of lecturing or master class work: the payback from the attendees who are in search of some knowledge or an experience makes this journey rewarding.

This e-book itself is a product of "love what you do." Many years of friends, acquaintances, and students telling me, "You should compile stories of your experiences over the years on that road to great performance, so the rest of us can gain by reading and understanding the journey," have led me to this point. So, as I sit here in my downstairs music room writing, I am continually telling myself to just do it for the reward at the end. Learning to write and getting the thoughts onto a page is the "practice" part. I'm creating this product the old school way here with a writing pad. There are ideas on the side, parts scrubbed out and started again, much like the starting and stopping of learning a new element for my sport or song/tune.

But hopefully soon there will be many pages of written material ready for "rehearsal." In writing, this would be called editing; in the journey to "great performance" I see it as parallel to Part Two : Rehearsal. We put all the ideas into a better order, fine tuning the products for performance, or in this case, delivering the product to the reader.

I do not consider myself a great writer by any means. But I "love what I do," which is to play, perform, and teach music. I can easily envision this book as a finished product, much like the music I compose or the music I am required to learn for events. My hope here is to give people some hope or knowledge and reassurance on their own journey. When you can remember and reinforce the fact that you love to do something (even through the hard-work days) and see in your mind's eye the finished product (which brings a smile to your face or those of others), then the laborious start of all that work does not seem so tough and demanding.

I'd like to tell you a story of the timeline at our house this past Boxing Day, December 26, 2015 that is all about "love what you do" and the "awesome performance."

Each year at our house, we host a large get-together of friends to celebrate the holiday season with a Boxing Day party. The crowd is very diverse, with people from different aspects of our lives. We have professional people from work, neighbours that come by, many students/ music friends and their families, and always a few new people, friends of others invited that come to the house. As a host, I get to talk to most people, and having several musicians in the house changes the flow of the party quite often.

To start the night's performing off, my wife Beverley played the fiddle and the Scottish small pipes (a quieter, in-house-type set of bagpipes in the key of A) along with one of her best pals on guitar. Beverley put many years of hard work into her playing years ago, and now, being very busy at her day job, she does not enjoy the work part (or the practice) so much. But she really does love to play the music, and it's a fantastic lesson for many of the other folks there. *It's not technically perfect but that doesn't matter as it is music and performance first and foremost.* This was a totally different form of "awesome performance." This "awesome performance" was inspiring to others. It showed other guests that this was not a recital competition at Carnegie Hall, but more a person up there playing music because they "love what they do" when they are playing.

So as the night progressed, all of the other players in the room got up to play as well. They all love what they do, but many are scared to show it at times for fear of imperfection. I understand that it is tough for many of these people to just play when myself or my son, Alex, is in the room, as we also teach many of them and we both demand a very high level of work at the lessons. But this was taking a break from perfection status and just entertaining people using our international language of music. We had veteran players performing tunes that they knew from memory of many years of playing years ago. Young kids (some after a bit of coaxing) played new tunes they were just learning. Some of our high-end competitive students, as well as myself and Alex, could step away from our current repertoire to just play tunes because we love to do it without the worry of mistakes hurting our reputations.

Beverley posted pictures of different performers onto social media, and the response from people literally around the world was incredible to read. From the west of us in Canada, to parts of the USA, Scotland, New Zealand, and Australia, people commented on how they wished they were here as well. They could "feel the music" coming out of those pictures, because they also "love what they do."

I've have often said "love what you do" and have often had a great experience of performance. But that night became special. I woke up halfway through the night and thoughts of this party would not stop rushing through my head. It was tough to get back to sleep. This was because for me, this wonderful example of "love what you do and do what you love" was fresh in my head and I knew this would be an experience that I would have to share in this book.

KEY TAKEAWAYS

❖ LOVE WHAT YOU DO—WHAT A FEELING!

❖ DO YOU LOVE IT ENOUGH THAT YOU CAN FEEL IT EMOTIONALLY?
   DOES IT MOTIVATE?

Your Personal Notes and Experiences

- What are your own reminders from this chapter?

....
....
....
....
....
....
....
....
....
....
....
....
....
....
....
....
....
....
....
....
....

For more information visit www.brucegandymusic.com

SECTION 3
Make It Fun

I've now been teaching for over thirty years at the time of writing this book. One of the key factors missing from several students trying to elevate their performance level is their ability to *make it fun*.

The skilled teachers will pass on methods to "make it fun" to their students to mix in with all of the hard training and exercise, which almost always results in a higher level of success. Within a band or a sports team, this tends to happen much easier, as the groups form up after a workout or rehearsal and then just play. Often, in sport, the team may separate into two groups by something as simple as a coin toss or names in alphabetical order. They proceed to take to the field and, while still trying hard, they play but perhaps no score is kept. Or if a player scores, they move to the other team. They just try to keep mixing things up and everyone has a great time at it.

Sometimes in a music ensemble they may start to play a piece that is not 100 percent rehearsed at all and just experiment. They may rotate who is singing lead or experiment with different instruments, just to get a different feel for it. So, instead of playing their practice pieces over and over for the upcoming show, they're taking time in between to have a little fun here. These wee breaks or experiments not only add fun and joy to the activity, they can also expose something very positive about a person's character or ability, and can also create something completely new and enjoyable.

The key here is to strike a balance between all of the hard work being done on exercises and drills, different plays or movements, and just going back to that inner child feeling where it is much easier to just make it fun and not worry so much about the result. Children try to win, but if they don't, well, they just come back tomorrow and try again.

The amount of time spent on doing work versus making it fun varies for each person or team. This depends on how serious the activity is meant to be and, very importantly, whether it is with children or adults. When people spend all of their time being so serious and technically perfect, their only thought is that end goal and it becomes very easy to lose sight of the process that is getting you there.

Children need to feel the difference between winning and fun. We have all heard stories in Canada of crazy hockey coaches trying to live out their dreams through the children's team. They have rules where the children need to be at practice five days a week as if they were in some elite military outfit. When some of the parents get on board with this thinking, it can become a nightmare. Documentaries have been made about these groups of people, and the experience can prove to be damaging in later life, as there is no balance with reality. Teams or players that get treated like this and lose have no self-esteem later on and often consider themselves to be losers later in life.

I have seen this type of person, sitting across the table from me in workshops and private lessons. Teams or players that only know winning often have a rough time when something new comes along and it throws them a curve ball. They cannot understand why they are not the very best, whether with music or sport, or even at work. They thought they were having fun because someone told them it was fun, but cannot recall the fun part of the journey that brought them to this place.

We've all heard the saying, "All work and no play makes . . ." So we must find balance between the hard work and the making it fun part.

Here is an example for me nowadays: There is another famous saying out there which is, "A bad day on the golf course still beats a good day at work." Of course, we know that this is a bit exaggerated, but the idea is something I try to follow all of the time now.

In high school I was a competitive golfer playing on a club team and scoring to about a four handicap (so, pretty serious when you think of it). But I also used to have friends who loved to play for fun in the neighbourhood. And we played a lot of golf on the street instead of on the course. We would have shots that had to bounce on the street, when aiming for the fence post, or aiming for the telephone pole, or a chip into a bucket. It was pure fun, nobody cared about scores, and I did not realize for many years the impact that this had on me. We grew up playing in the streets and it was important who golfed best, or scored the most goals in road hockey, or ran the fastest playing soccer or baseball, but it was only important until the next time we played. I can easily visualize in my mind to this day some of the shots or holes we designed on our street course. At the same time, I can remember the names of my friends who always played. *But* I cannot remember who hit the telephone pole the most times or scored that winning goal, because we all had a great time doing it, and it actually made us better players.

What is important to me is that now I still love to be out on the golf course. It takes me away from the hustle and stress that even a great job like I have still has, and many anxieties are just forgotten about. I try to be realistic with golf now. I'm not competitive and I play to a thirteen or so handicap. But I make it fun now. I try to understand the limitations, and for me I've taken out as much competitiveness (I think) as I can. What I tell people now is, "I don't care how many shots I take in the end. As long as I'm hitting the ball and not spending all day looking for it, that's good."

Some folks in society are starting to shift their way of thinking and they try to make everything "fun" for the teams. The players learn that it is not always about the result. Rather, it is much more about the journey and the participation that makes it fun. *Whatever form of awesome you are aiming for, there is a balance between the hard work, hard practice, hard exercise, and the fun work, fun practice, and fun exercise.* Too much of one can of these can overpower the other.

I have had the great fortune to work with several adults in my time. Accountants, electricians, labourers, pilots, doctors, bulldozer operators, seminar and think tank leaders, ministers and priests, former pro athletes, and many firemen and police officers, to name just a few. When adults start to pay money for lessons, many of them need to see that return on investment quickly. Some just want to get into a band for the camaraderie, and others miss that competitive feeling they used to experience as a child. Many of these professional people work hard at this but do not get the result they expect, as they are used to succeeding.

In my work as a bagpipe teacher I have to constantly look for ways to make the practice fun for the player. The idea of just coming to their lesson, doing drills for an hour on their technical side, and then practicing for a week before the next session can grow stale very quickly. My job is to teach them the correct methods, but also to put fun into this. Making exercises into a game for each exercise can help, but may still not be enough. Some musicians do not live close enough to belong to a group and that can create a bit of boredom on their part. I try to get these musicians to actively pursue a venue or gig where they can perform. This way, they work hard at home with a bit of a defined purpose, sometimes making a game of the work or imagining themselves playing on some fancy stage. If they let people know what they are trying to do, after a bit of word-of-mouth advertising they may find themselves performing at a senior's home, for example. There's no first prize at this event; the prize is seeing the smiles of joy on the people's faces when you perform. Of course there is still some pressure here, if you care about your reputation. But all that work and rehearsal at home now feels right, because you were able to "make it fun."

KEY TAKEAWAYS

❖ FOCUS—WHAT ARE YOUR DISTRACTIONS?

❖ EXPERIMENT SOME DAYS BY JUST INVENTING A GIG WHERE YOU WILL PLAY.

❖ MAKE A GAME OUT OF TECHNICAL EXERCISES.

❖ FIND THE BALANCE BETWEEN STRICT WORK AND FUN REHEARSAL.

❖ ARE YOU PRACTICING CONCENTRATION?

❖ HAVE SOME FUN!

❖ ARE YOU MAKING TIME FOR YOUR INNER CHILD IN REHEARSAL?

Your Personal Notes and Experiences

- What are your own reminders from this chapter?

....

....

....

....

....

....

....

....

....

....

....

....

....

....

....

....

....

....

For more information visit www.brucegandymusic.com

Develop Confidence in Yourself

*The artist who aims for perfection in everything
achieves it in nothing.*

—*Eugene*

Whether you are a musician, or an athlete rehearsing for the next event, you must develop a checklist and action plan to monitor the progress of your instrument or body. With young people, this may be as easy as having them write down the amount of time spent practicing their discipline. This leads to a start in accountability.

Once you become a bit older or more advanced, we are then looking to refine this process to help bring you to awesome performance. From this point on in the chapter, I will be using descriptions for the bagpipe, but you can draw comparisons to other activities yourself. Developing confidence and actually really understanding what you are doing are two very different ideals, and the higher the skill level that you reach the more effort is required to manage yourself at that level. If we look at three very basic levels of the bagpipe performer, we can see how the confidence and performing level change as you progress into this rehearsal stage.

Beginner: For the beginner to be able to perform with any kind of confidence, this person has to put enough physical practice (as directed by their coach) to actually stand up on the stage and play to the end of the piece in some recognizable form. Some beginners are über-positive players that seem to own the world when they perform. They are confident, but often do not possess a good ability to evaluate their own performance for errors, and this can be both helpful and harmful: helpful in that they do not overthink the process and just get on with it, and harmful in that this can develop a situation where the player is trying to progress but has a few bad habits and does not have the discipline to fix them. This is where the coach is so vital in helping to strike a good balance.

Intermediate: This is a big step forward for many musicians. The intermediate musician should now be starting to hear the difference between just blowing and making noise, and having the instrument sounding pleasant and "in tune."

There are many other books describing the complexities of the instrument, so this is not the place for that. However, it is important to realize that, at this stage, it is not just moving a drone or two into place and the instrument being ready like a guitar might be. The intermediate musician is now starting to realize that in order to make the bagpipe sound pleasant, they must be able to deal with *tuning all three drones together with the melody chanter.*

The player must also start to understand the bag itself and the aspects of controlling the moisture content and humidity that is in the climate where they are playing. This will take more practice time in each session, so the player can work on both the fingering of the piece and the sound of the instrument. The players will still need help from their coaches to make the instrument sound better, but each small step they take to sharpen or flatten a note or drone successfully develops tremendous confidence.

I get to hear a lot of intermediate performers at competitions throughout the year. When you hear someone trying to sound better and listening hard to the sound of their instrument as they try to make minor adjustments, their playing, in general, combined with their focus, is much more confident nine times out of ten.

On the other side of the equation, performers who "just play" without even trying to tune often suffer in their presentation of the music. You ask them how they played and invariably get, "It was terrible! I started out great, but something happened to the pipes and it was really distracting so I ended up making a couple of big mistakes." There are times when you have to downplay this, as the person was trying hard. Maybe you ask questions about their preparation for the event, from that day to even the few days that led up to it. Other times, if you have worked with someone to start tuning and sounding their instrument better and they do nothing on the day that parallels their practice, you then need to evaluate why this is happening. Neither one of these players has performed with much confidence at all. The resulting poor performance will also hurt their confidence the next time they perform in front of a judge or audience.

Advanced: *When I talk with my peers about performance preparation and confidence, almost all of them tell me the secret to a good performance is to be in good form, physically and mentally prior to the event.* But more important is that you are in control of the variables. There are always differences that occur between your practice area and the performance area. When you are well prepared and make the changes necessary to deal with the room, or the wind on the golf course, perhaps, you develop more confidence as you are "owning the situation at hand." When you are advanced in any sport or musical form, you should be well practiced in all of the basic disciplines.

When I coach my advanced musicians, I do not teach them the note on a score. They come to me knowing the musical notes with an instrument sounding well enough to be used in live performance. They should be well-practiced and well-rehearsed, in order to be confident in what they are doing. They may be slightly unsure if their delivery is going to be perfectly accurate, but I try to get them to just commit to what they feel right then.

As an aside, it's almost hypocritical of me to coach like that, as "lack of commitment" is one of my own top faults on a golf course nowadays. This is much different than my competitive years on the golf teams in high school.

If you commit to the shot you are taking, or the music score you are playing, you develop consistency in your approach and confidence begins to grow in your approach. Now, if the coach happens to see or hear something that they feel could elevate the performance, it is much easier to tweak slightly. The coach can suggest just a small alteration to their swing, their stance, or a musical phrase, which can have a dramatic effect on the outcome. Once the player is back in control of this small action, the result becomes better and this elevates the confidence once again for the player.

I am reminded of a small speech, turned into a video from PGA golf pro Graeme McDowell, MBE from Northern Ireland. Simply called, "The Journey to Better," this should be required viewing for any athlete or musician, if only the first twenty-five seconds.

In this video at the start there is a quote:

"There's never really a 'good enough' in golf, there's always better. The search for perfection in a game that is really imperfectable. So, I guess we're always on the Journey to Better. Negativity is a part of human instinct. It's important to realize that's okay. Let that in, replace that with good positivity, good ideas, visualizations, and good feelings. (https://www.youtube.com/watch?v=6CoVE-UN9G4&t=2s)

KEY TAKEAWAYS

❖ YOU MAY BE CONFIDENT, BUT DO YOU UNDERSTAND WHAT YOU ARE DOING?

❖ MAKE THE INSTRUMENT SOUND BETTER TO HELP ELEVATE YOUR PERFORMANCE.

❖ CONSISTENCY AND REPETITION OF ANY SINGLE ELEMENT HELPS TO BREED A HIGHER LEVEL OF CONFIDENCE.

Your Personal Notes and Experiences

- What are your own reminders from this chapter?

....

....

....

....

....

....

....

....

....

....

....

....

....

....

....

....

....

....

....

For more information visit www.brucegandymusic.com

SECTION 5
Prepare for Competition/Performance

When the instrument (body) is working and the
discipline is 100 percent, only then can the delivery
be to its full potential.

—Bruce Gandy

Preparing yourself properly for an event can, in most cases, be as important as the event itself. The skilled professional generally has a routine in which he or she goes through automatically, but in my experience as a teacher I have found that each and every step towards the optimum performance must be carefully explained and instilled into the memory of the student, no matter what age he or she may be.

Many students will be able to pick up some of the tricks by watching and asking questions of the premier performers. Others will not have the ability to do this, so it must be taught.

All too often I have seen this scenario: A person walks shyly up to the platform or stage and mumbles out a few words about what selection of music they intend to perform for you. Then they stand back about ten feet and get ready for the scariest two minutes of their life. Standing at attention or rigid, they sound the instrument, and proceed right into the tune as soon as both arms are on the bagpipe. They have not practiced in front of people or even marched (in the case of a bagpiper) at home or in lessons, so whatever rhythm they had is now lost because they are now marching aimlessly along to a tune, looking at the audience or judge as if seeking approval that they have gone far enough one way, now it's time to turn the other way. It's no wonder they are scared. Without some sort of pre-event routine, they have no idea what to do, and I'm sure you can guess what their level of confidence will be.

I am sure that a lot of people have seen this sort of situation. I believe that with good tuition the minor problems can be easily fixed, so the person has a better grasp of what he or she is doing. The reason I say these issues are easy to solve is simply because I have seen the youngest of children marching up to the platform like they own the world, and it is very impressive.

There is always an argument from folks who say, "He's just a young person performing for the first time and he's barely been playing for six months with a new piece. How is he to be expected to remember all that?" Of course, you cannot expect everything in a day, but there are some things that can be learned easily and others that will take longer.

In preparing a person who is going into their first performance, I feel a couple of steps can be successfully used to ease some of the nervousness.

Assuming the basic learning of the music is done, (Part One : Practice), a person can move forward. This means you must be absolutely familiar with the music and comfortable enough with the memory that you can now move to the next phase of preparation.

Part Two : Rehearsal: As we have been talking about in this chapter, it is imperative that the performer has a daily routine which they follow. *Constantly sticking to the routine develops a rhythm in your work, which develops habit, and in turn begins to develop confidence.*

Here are some things you can consider in the rehearsal phase that will help you get ready for the "Big Event":

ROLE PLAYING

This procedure is used all through your competitive and performing years, but is also most important in the early stages. What I suggest is that the coach sits at the table with a pen and paper and you (the student) play for them just as if it was Saturday morning at the contest or the Friday night recital at the conservatory. Starting off in the other room, the coach may help tune up the instrument, and make sure that the components of the instrument are in good working order.

(Note: While the student is warming up, the coach should be giving reassurance that everything is okay in order to instill confidence. Don't give someone trouble right before the event because they didn't practice enough last week or they're missing out on some technical area. This is not the time for that. Now is the time to put the performer at ease.)

Now, the performer enters the staged area (the basement, for example) and proceeds towards the table. This is what you should do: You should be walking proudly with the instrument on your shoulders or in your arms. Don't lumber along with your instrument like a child dragging his school bag down the hall. *Stand up straight, introduce yourself, and speak clearly when announcing what you are going to perform.* Don't whisper!

When the judge/audience is ready, turn around and get yourself ready. Take your time and relax. When blowing up your bagpipes, for instance, do not sound the chanter until the bag is under your arm and both hands are clearly on the chanter in proper position, as it otherwise looks terrible and sounds awful.

You should have learned a few tuning notes or phrases to play to get yourself relaxed for a few seconds before you start your tune. Now your instrument has hopefully settled back into tune and you are ready to start playing. The more you go through these rehearsals, the better you will be on the day of the event. You must have full concentration for the time it takes to play the piece, and if you can picture yourself on the platform, you will be much better off when the time comes for the real event.

I would not suggest going as far as dress rehearsals at lessons, but just remember to look smart when you play. Simple things like a nice tie, a well-ironed uniform, and other neat and tidy accessories really make a difference and show that you care. These few things not only prepare you to play with a bit more ease, they also begin to teach you proper ways to rehearse.

Assuming that you have reached a higher level of skill, I would like to look at some of the tips and techniques of preparation and how to use them.

NERVES AND CONFIDENCE

Are you rehearsed enough that you are ready to give a good, sound performance?

Having talked about this with many different performers, most agree that the best chance of getting rid of nerves is to be prepared solidly. James MacGillivray, a Gold Medal winner, says this of his own preparation:

"I feel that as soon as winning or playing well becomes important, the nerves start to show through. If you are just out to have fun, then naturally, you won't be affected by nerves as much. For example, if I know that the last ten times I played over the piece it was very good with no errors, I am confident that I am ready to perform this in public."

It is critical to be honest with yourself. One of the real problems of competitive playing is that the competitor doesn't realize how well or how poorly they are playing (hope versus expectation). In this situation, it is advisable to not only record yourself at home and on the field, but to also find another person whom you really trust and respect, and listen to their opinion. Maybe you thought one of your pieces, for instance, was just fine, but when a few people start telling you that you are playing too fast, don't just say, "I don't think so." Listen to the recording and listen to their opinion.

FATIGUE

Although playing bagpipes or other instruments may not be classified as an athletic event, it is a performance requiring at times a lot of physical strength and mental concentration. Fatigue can become an important factor in playing.

For instance, if you are playing in some summer events, you may have three to four solo events, plus a band contest, all in one day. As a bagpiper, consider the extreme heat of playing with a black jacket and hat, the possibility of playing for a drumming event, the opening ceremonies to perform at, and an average one hour tune up to prepare all of the different people and corps for the band contest. A person will most likely be very worn out before the band steps on to the field. As soon as you get tired, you begin to lose concentration and the mistakes suddenly start to reappear.

Everyone is affected in some way by fatigue, some more than others. If you are in good shape and you are health conscious, a day like this may not try you as much. On the other hand, the stress may wear you out to a point that you think you are going to collapse.

Take advantage of any time you get to relax and use it wisely. Drink water. Eat. Rest up. Don't wear your heavy clothing all day if it is hot. Spend time visualizing instead of playing. Chat with others and get it into your head that this is just another day, an opportunity to perform, even an exciting one. But take care of yourself and pace yourself.

MUSIC SELECTION

No matter how young or old or how proficient or inexperienced you may be, proper music selection for your competition/performance is very important if you want to have any success at all.

There are a great many things to consider when picking the right piece but the most important one is *do not play music which is too difficult!* The goal in a contest is to play your very best and to give yourself the best chance to win the prize. Why play a piece where technique and musicality are beyond your capabilities when you know that you can make a very nice job of a much easier tune?

The other big issue I see with lower grade players is that they barely have a tune memorized and already they want to compete with it. This is competitive suicide.

Why not play a piece of music that you learned some time ago, one you are quite sure that you can make a good job of? Not only will you have a much better chance of success, you probably won't be as nervous as you would be playing a new piece. You will have more confidence.

Picking music at a higher level takes a lot of evaluation if you want the right selection. Some players have what you might call a very heavy-handed big technical style and might pick music that is technically heavy to suit their skills. Others might play a light-handed piece, allowing more freedom of interpretation. This is a very broad comparison, but the point is that some pieces of music, even if you like them, may or may not suit your playing. The trick is to find out either by recording yourself or taking someone else's opinion and deciding which music best suits you. *After a while, skilled or experienced players will usually know which tunes they can play to best enhance the musicality of the tune.* I still play music for my own mentors to get their opinion on that one aspect, musicality. (Not whether I'm executing perfectly or not, but just getting a general feel for it.)

TECHNIQUE

Depending on your level of skill, technique will also play a deciding role in picking music. Getting control of the technical handwork is one of the biggest stepping stones to developing good music. It has to be clear and consistent, and there is no better way to achieve this than by playing exercises. The rule of thumb which I was taught is quite simple:

Learn how to play the exercise properly then be honest with yourself. Don't try to play the exercise ten times over, occasionally letting yourself off the hook. Just try to play it once correctly.

If you can do this, your ability and control will be better, and there is a much greater chance of not making an error in the tune.

INSTRUMENT

One of the most important factors in producing a good performance is the ability to produce a good sounding instrument. In a bagpipe competition for instance, good tone can account for up to 50 percent of your total score, and an unstable instrument can also knock you right out of the contest.

The real fact, though, is simple: Nobody likes to listen to anyone playing on an out-of-tune instrument. You have to make sure that you know how your instrument is going to react. Most of what you need to know should be covered in a maintenance session, but I'll just point out a few things to look for when getting instrument (in this case, the bagpipe) ready to compete with.

First of all, if you are struggling to blow the bagpipe steady, this will not only hurt your tonal quality, but your concentration of the music will also suffer. Make sure that you check the pipe bag for leaks by corking up the stocks and seeing if any air leaks through.

If the bag appears to be fine, check all of the hemped up drone slides to make sure that the hemp has not dried out and lost its grip (this is a common problem if your pipes have not been played very regularly).

Then check the chanter reed to make sure that it is not too stiff and lacking in vibration.

Last of all, a big problem in blowing a hard bagpipe is that the drone reeds are taking too much air. Getting the drone reeds just right takes a long time to master, as moisture has such a great effect on them. Remember this: just because the reeds were fine last week doesn't mean they will be fine next time. Get yourself into the habit of checking each individual reed before you play.

SUMMARY

Now that you have picked your music and practiced hard and your instrument is sounding well, are you ready to perform/compete? The answer is: almost.

First of all, have you developed any stage craft yet? This would include your entrance and exit to the performance area and perhaps how you deal with the crowd. While mostly a musical scenario, this also applies to sport, from golf or dancing to horse racing. Giving some of your personality out in a good positive way will enhance the situation for any viewer and increase your own confidence once again. If you have not considered this, watch some of the veterans in your field and ask your coach how to practice this at home. After performing a few times, this should become much more familiar.

Have you thought about post-event interviews as well?

There are thousands of musicians playing endless types of different tuning notes, phrases, chords, or speech pattern and none of them are right or wrong. Listen and watch others to get a feel for it, and then try to create your own style. Get some help making them up if need be. The only guideline that you need to follow, if any, is that these warm up tunes should be pleasant to listen to. The best way to check this is to record yourself and listen with friends to decide if they meet your standards. This helps to put yourself, a judge, or an audience at ease before you officially start your piece.

The last thing to look at is the ability to focus. I feel this is extremely important in practice, and when used properly it will be successful. It is no secret that athletes around the world focus on their task while practicing and envision themselves scoring, sinking the putt, making the highest jump, winning the race, etc. When you can see yourself performing beautifully up on the stage, you will begin to believe in yourself and thus overcome those two big obstacles to success: having confidence to know that you can perform well, and controlling your nerves. When you have already seen yourself play great several times and you are sure that you are going to do well, you can begin to think, "What is there to worry about?"

I never coach any of my students on how to win. That's just too much pressure on the player. Instead I coach them to perform to their best, their own "world's best" so they do not lose within their own selves. Yes, another performer, or athlete, may finish better or score higher, but you are not in control of their situation. *If you have practiced and rehearsed with commitment and purpose, you can perform with confidence and passion.* If you perform very well, then you have done all you can and have now put the pressure on the others to do better.

KEY TAKEAWAYS

❖ FOLLOW YOUR PLAN.

❖ YOU CANNOT ADVANCE IF YOU DON'T COMMIT TO THE PROCESS.

❖ OWN THAT REHEARSAL STAGE.

❖ STAND TALL AND CONFIDENT, NO MATTER WHERE YOU ARE.

❖ BE AT ONE WITH YOURSELF.

❖ REHEARSE TO PERFORM WITHIN YOUR OWN LEVEL.

Your Personal Notes and Experiences

- What are your own reminders from this chapter?

....

....

....

....

....

....

....

....

....

....

....

....

....

....

....

....

....

....

....

For more information visit www.brucegandymusic.com

PART THREE
Performance

78th Highlander performance—North American Championships 2017.

You have learned the tunes by studying them intently, practicing with a purpose, recording yourself, and going the extra mile to really know the material. You have rehearsed, building up your confidence, visualizing the circumstances in which you will be presenting your tunes, even going so far as to create a mock environment to help eliminate as many potential distractions.

The *next* step in the Total Preparation Package is the performance itself and what you can do to be ready to share with your audience (whether they are friends, family, recital attendees, or judges).

This is the time you've been waiting for, the moment when all your hard work comes together to share with the world all that you've learned. But maybe you are nervous or anxious. Maybe you are losing your concentration or have lost that feeling of confidence and joy and the motivation to play. Here, I introduce you to the *One-eighty Factor*—a method I created to help you get mentally prepared *for the day* by preventing you from focusing negatively on the "problems" and instead forcing you to identify *issues and their solutions.*

Performance summary.

SECTION 1
One-Eighty Factor

The *One-eighty Factor* is a name which describes a very simple process I have developed and used for many years in my coaching classes.

Have you ever found yourself up on stage performing or on the first tee at a golf tournament with all sorts of odd feelings? Your body feels all tight and in rigid muscular tension. Maybe your stomach is getting the better of you. It feels like everything that you have practiced and rehearsed for has gone out the window and you only have negative fears and thoughts left. Well, the good news is that you are not alone, and there're ways to help combat this distractive feeling.

When I am coaching, and I ask my players to review their performance, I usually get one of two common answers. The first one sounds something like, "I played very well and I don't think I missed anything. I'm not sure why I didn't win, I thought it was pretty excellent. That other person had a couple little slips that I heard so I don't know."

What this person has done in their own performance (generalizing here) is just play some notes with rigid concentration and is unaware of the other factors that come into account. I listen to their summary and then proceed to ask a few questions.

The second player, when asked, has been concentrating and listening and they tell me every little thing that went wrong with their performance. "I was going fine until I had a slip in Part Two . Then I think I sped up a little later on. I didn't know it was going to be so much hotter on the platform than in the warm up area and my instrument went way out of tune." Or any other of several excuses for their less-than-stellar performance. It's easy if you can answer all the reasons why the performance or game didn't go as planned. You have just justified it all to yourself, which seems to make it all okay.

I hear this on a weekly basis from many of the people I coach after their competitions take place. You can accept loss now because you know all the issues that occurred. You have talked yourself into thinking it's okay. There are errors and you know what they were, so surely it will not happen the next time.

In these two scenarios, neither person has accepted the fact that the other players' music or sport technique was just better. Sure, they knocked the ball in the water on the fourteenth hole, but they may have steadied up for the rest of the round and produced a great score.

One of the interesting things I always hear when golfers are being interviewed is that they think and relate to the good points in their round. Due to their coaching, they know to stay positive and build on their strength.

Not long ago I heard a top pro speaking after a very shaky opening round. It went something like this, "I don't feel the score is reflective of how we played today. I hit the ball very good and consistent today. But the wind came up today off of the water and I made a few wrong club selections hitting into the greens. If you don't get on the correct side of the pins or on the green itself is very difficult to get up and down for those pars. We will just go back to the range, make a few adjustments, and study the yardage book a little bit better. I'm putting the ball very well right now, so if I can do a bit better job of getting myself in position, we should be able to make up some ground there." The next day he shot sixty-five and was right up near the top of the leaderboard.

The point here is twofold: He did not dwell on what went wrong, and he figured out why some of the things were not as good as they could have been. This is a very positive mindset. It's thinking in the form of the old saying that the bottle is half full versus half empty. If a person receives some imaginary score of, say, ninety points, the bottle-half-empty thinkers only see the errors and deductions. The bottle-half-full thinkers see the score, or rating, or position that they've achieved during the performance and find all the good points first. Then, their thought pattern says that if they tried this or that, or focused more here or there, this could easily have been up past the personal best range they set for themselves. So, they go back to the practice range or the studio, work on these perceived faults to try to eliminate them, and insert the newly corrected versions into the rest of the good performance.

One-eighty Factor is my system that I use to coach all my musicians. It stems from years of personal development and reading and has been a turning point for my own game as a competitive musician and performer. The actual process is simple and nothing more than a paper, pencil, and your brain. The trick is in the execution of the process.

First, take a sheet of paper. Draw a line across the top, and a line down the middle. Over the left column write "the Issue." Over the right column, write "the Solution."

Now, write down every "issue" you have identified in the performance. Maybe it is an obstacle, maybe it is a technique, maybe it is a circumstance, maybe it is a specific part of the music, maybe it is the instrument. I try to avoid using the word "problem," as that has a very negative tone. These are not "problems," they are "issues" that have concrete actions that can be taken to fix them, to help you on the way toward "Delivering Your Own Awesome."

As you have probably anticipated by now, the right side of the sheet is where you address each of these issues. You create a concrete action plan addressing the specific item you've identified.

Here is an example of a student's One-eighty Factor chart:

The Issue	The Solution
Scared to perform in front of a large crowd of unfamiliar faces	- Learn to embrace the crowd. - If they are better performers than you, they will respect your effort. If they are not as experienced, they will most likely not hear small differences. - Find more opportunities to perform in front of others, so you can get used to it.
It's so hot compared to the practice room	- Keep a towel handy. - Find a shady place. - Stay hydrated at all times.
It's a new venue. Where do I go?	- Plan to arrive early to get used to your surroundings.
There are food tables with generators and many other performers nearby distracting.	- Focus on your own tuning, not the generator or other performers. If you do a reasonable job, the judge will be impressed with your effort (and probably can't hear you very well over the noise anyway).
What if it rains?	- Find a dry place and stay there until the last moment. - Be careful walking to and on the platform.
I never get a prize from this judge	- Do not play "for" the judge. Play "at" the judge, as if showing them how it is "meant" to be played.

Those are just a few of the issues that may occur, and in fact, we dug much deeper into this later on in this student's lesson. I asked the person to write more, leaving nothing out if possible. This will vary tremendously depending on the event or venue that you may be attending, and the person that you are working with, but this example gives you a general idea of how the One-eighty Factor works.

You may find that the issues you state are too broad, almost an umbrella topic. In this case you will find that you have to subdivide that issue into several smaller issues. For example, just saying it's hot out is very broad. You may have a large checklist to help you offset the issues you face from the heat.

When you write down every issue you feel you are facing and then work on each of these with the potential solution or action idea, seeing your own positive outcome, your confidence will rise and you'll give yourself a chance to perform at a peak, world best level.

For some people, they find it even more powerful to have three columns on their paper.

Column one describes the issue being faced.

Column two is the solution, or action needed

Column three is actually writing the result they will feel when this is achieved. Although it may seem obvious, there is much written that seeing that result written or score marked down helps the confidence as well.

I have read that the power of journaling can be life-altering for some people. To read your own words and become self-aware can become a major tool in your personal transformation, be it a reminder to save money or your progress in exercising or even a bigger life goal. When you actually see the words, you can respond easier and/or break the goals down into manageable pieces.

Writing something down deepens the commitment and helps keep the task in focus for success!

The reasoning behind the One-eighty Factor is to help find concrete answers for sometimes nebulous and worrying issues. It is also a very good tool to bridge the gap between what you do at home and what you do on the performance platform or stage, field, arena, or course.

Most people, myself included, cannot get a real true grasp of why everything is so different between home and the live event. It's very easy to lay blame on all scenarios that you feel you cannot control. For example, one easy reason we hear is the weather/venue change. It's too hot or it was very cold or windy or very noisy. All of these give you mental justification for your worry or your eventual (poor) performance, and they seem to make it okay. What you *need* to be searching for here are as many clues to unlock your fight-or-flight instinct or perhaps your hope-versus-expectation reality. *You must gain a realization of what is out there so that you can convert these deficits and move toward your own personal best each time.*

I am a very lucky man to have spent a lot of time with my father-in-law for almost thirty years before his untimely passing. He was a father to me, also a friend. We played on the dart team at the local pub, and we also played golf together. We spent many years playing the pipes together in a world championship band. We also did jobs together as adjudicators at different competition venues. But he was also a joiner and building contractor and he put me through my apprenticeship as a carpenter in my twenties.

Pipe Major Ronald G Rollo, father-in-law, mentor, judge, and friend.
Photo credit June Rollo

He had many great stories and anecdotes and I am forever thankful for this training that I received as a result. Part of this great training is the story that I would like to share with you. This is still so clear in my mind thirty years on that it really was a life-changing event. I just didn't know it at the time.

I believe it was in my final year of apprenticing as a carpenter and the crew were all working for a while on the restoration of a very big old mansion, well in excess of one hundred years old. I had become reasonably good at trim and finishing work and very much enjoyed that part of the job. Some liked the start of the job, as they felt the new life they were bringing up from the ground. Others enjoyed the middle of the jobs after the framing was finished and all of the different trades were there. But being a bit of an introvert, I enjoyed the quiet of working on my own. But more important, I enjoyed this phase because it was finishing the woodwork in the house. I needed to think hard to make the angles work on all sorts of trim, casing windows, doors, shelving, etc. And it was never just as it should be in the book.

On this particular job, all of the doors had to be changed out. Twenty-four or twenty-five in total. I was tasked to install all these doors. Normally this job wouldn't be too difficult, as door frames were properly put in place and with a bit of careful measuring everything moved along nicely. But in this house, over a century old, the frames were original we were not allowed to touch those. All that I had learned working with the new doors during my apprenticeship and schooling was null and void for this job.

What a struggle! I only knew the procedure and the ABC rules of hanging doors. So, being worried that I would be in trouble for not getting much done so far, I gathered all my verbal ammunition to tell my father-in-law/boss why I was not that far along with the doors. I remember saying, "These frames are all out of whack, nothing is plumb, nothing level, door jams are not square. Some doors are way too big to fit into the jams as well." All of the justification in the world to say why it didn't work.

He took it all in and then looked at me and said in this regular Scottish accent, "Listen, pal, hanging these doors is what you get paid for, and while school teaches you the procedures and the theory, it's not always the same as the real thing. Let me tell you this and listen clearly and think about this: There's naebody that complains about a door that works. *So dinnae give me all the problems pal; I need the solutions.*"

That was really where my vision of the One-eighty Factor began to take shape: not focusing on the problems, but finding the solutions. But I didn't realize the power of that statement for another eight to ten years, when I began to use this in my own musical performing and coaching.

Whether you are playing golf, hockey, or music, you first have to realize and acknowledge that things are different physically, mentally and even spiritually between the practice area and the performance area. You must prepare yourself for the different elements of the live performance. Once you are completely in sync with your task, you can turn the negative thoughts or distractions around and work it to your advantage. In performance, this can turn a routine, technical display into a performance which is much more appealing to the audience to both view and to feel. In a competition, being in control of yourself and adapting to the elements can give you a tremendous edge over fellow competitors.

One last example occurred as a bit of luck for me and terrible luck for a fellow colleague at a very prestigious event in Scotland. Each year, the top ten winners of the most prestigious bagpipe events through the year are invited to compete on the last Saturday of October. The venue for the performance is the great hall of the prestigious Blair Castle, just outside Pitlochry, Scotland. Everything about the event is first class, and it is a stunning setting. But the competition itself is a very high-pressure, packed event.

The camaraderie between players at this event is truly amazing. Of course, each person wants to do their own world best and win the event, but each competitor is also absolutely respectful and encouraging to the fellow players. My first time at the event, I was just so happy to get that support when I was literally shaking out of my boots there.

The stage in the great hall is just raised up perhaps sixteen inches and the wall behind is covered in stags' heads, swords, and paintings of famous folk there. To say "intimidating" would be putting it lightly.

There are also a couple of windows which look out onto the very beautiful grounds and can help to bring a sense of peace to it all. On this one year, one of the players was up playing a great classical piece, full focus and concentration on a beautiful sounding instrument which resonated throughout the room perfectly.

Anyway, on this day, halfway through the performance, a big peacock jumped up on the window ledge as the performer turned that way and the bird opened up its plumage wide to display its beautiful colours. This sudden shock threw the player's mind out of line for a moment and he lost his place in the piece and had to stop. Something we never want to face, ever.

I felt terrible for my friend and co-competitor, but I stepped outside and immediately knew that I needed to put my own One-eighty Factor training into effect. I thought about that performance, the room, the bird, everything, and then proceeded to envision myself there. My advantage is that now I actually knew that this could happen once again, and I needed to make sure that I could handle it under pressure. As I warmed up, I thought about it a couple of times, but just in a "reminder" sort of way. As I stepped onto the stage to ready myself, I warmed up with a bit of a slow piece just to settle myself and the crowd before commencing into the required piece I had been asked to play. I wandered toward the window and could see the birds there and I just stared them down for a few moments, telling myself in my head that it was okay, they were outside. They might come up and make some noise but I thought, Just see them, recognize it, and don't let it distract you from the tune.

This worked wonderfully, and I gained a very high prize in that event that day. It was another real sign of proof that taking a situation and applying the One-eighty Factor to it greatly increases the chance of success.

KEY TAKEAWAYS

❖ THERE ARE NO "PROBLEMS," THERE ARE "ISSUES."

❖ EVERY "ISSUE" HAS A SOLUTION—YOU JUST NEED TO FIND IT!

❖ USE THE ONE-EIGHTY FACTOR TO HELP YOU IDENTIFY LARGE SOLUTIONS;
BREAK THEM DOWN TO SMALLER ITEMS YOU CAN MANAGE AND SOLVE.

❖ JOURNALING: WRITING IT DOWN DEEPENS THE COMMITMENT.

❖ LIFE LESSONS: "DINNAE GIVE ME YOUR PROBLEMS, PAL,
I NEED SOLUTIONS."

Your Personal Notes and Experiences

- What are your own reminders from this chapter?

....
....
....
....
....
....
....
....
....
....
....
....
....
....
....
....
....
....
....
....

For more information visit www.brucegandymusic.com

SECTION 2
Visualization

Success in music requires hard work and discipline.
If you are not afraid of the initial failures,
then the opportunities are endless.

—Bruce Gandy

Visualization is a term that gets bounced around in music and sport often, but in reality it takes many years to master. I first learned the term watching Olympic weightlifters. As a young boy I thought this was all part of the act of these huge powerful men.

Sure, this would add an exciting element to the person's performance, instead of just walking up to a bar, picking up the weight, then dropping it back to the mat with a thunderous crash. Okay, I was young and naïve. But one day, I got lucky, as a coach was on with the television announcer and he began to explain this part of the preparation. The coach explained how visualization was every bit as important as the lift itself on competition day. This is not just make-believe, fairy tale imagination stuff. In fact, it may look like that at the start, but in the end it is an incredible exercise and display of focus. These giants have their minds in tune so well that they can do superhuman world best lifts that they have not achieved before, right when the pressure is greatest for them.

Adrenaline is an amazing hormone and neurotransmitter (also known as epinephrine). This is produced by the adrenal gland located at the top of the kidneys. When a stressful situation occurs, adrenaline is released into blood, which sends signals to the organs.

I'm sure many people have heard of the fight-or-flight response and witnessed personally, or have seen on television, incredible acts of strength or courage. One example would be seeing a person moving a great weight or even lifting a car up so another can be rescued. These are super human acts and a person could not normally do this.

What the weight lifter does is use incredible focus and real visualization, which can get them in that same type of adrenaline-inducing trance. They do not think of numbers and pounds; they only see the huge weight attached to the bar and they understand the process that needs to occur. When you watch the athlete finally step up to the bar, the focus is incredible. He is in a different state of mind, and has the ability to do something that most people would see as impossible.

I became fascinated with this process and after a few highly disastrous personal performances, began to study the process in small steps to try to channel some of this negative "flight" hormone and turn it into a positive "fight" hormone.

One step to visualization is to have a real sense of reality in understanding the difference between hope and expectation. (This is something we get into later on.) You have to take a step back and remember what you *can* do, *not* what you all of a sudden *think* you can do.

Kathleen Zinck, a champion curler who has represented Nova Scotia nine times at the National championship and played in the World Final, had this to say about visualization and focus:

Bruce, I am a big fan of visualization. When I get in the car to drive to the club I start to visualize my surroundings there. I picture the shots I am going to make, and see a good outcome. If I am travelling to another club, I always go right to the club, observe where spectators will be, the type of hacks they have (what you put your foot in to push off, although now they are all standardized). I would take a look at the type of roof in the rink, listen to the acoustics, and how sound travels when the players call out. We also use hand signals when we can't be heard. I check out the temperature in the ice shed as many clubs are much colder than arenas so you have to dress in different layers. I would always try to find and talk with the ice makers for patterns in their ice, how high they put the pebble on and when the pebbles usually start to break down, and again visualize making shots.

When at Nationals I would always do this in all of the arenas I played at, as the ice makers have so much more to battle with. They only get the ice surface for a short time in the week before a competition to change the surface from hockey to curling ice. The ice makers in the arenas also have so much more training in ice making than in local clubs.

I need to be able to focus entirely on the game, or tournament. In curling on a team, my teammates would have no idea if I had just left an ill child at home or failed to help them with a school assignment. Once I left the house, I tried to leave the mom at home and just focus on the match. I did up a contract and made each player sign it if they wanted to curl with me.

My three other players had never won a Provincial but I had this visualization that we would win, and we did.

When you are curling, sometimes the pin (middle of the circle) feels so small to draw to and other times so large and easy to land on. When it is small, you take a step back and change your self-thought, bringing you back to a much more confident visualization.

I would like to share a couple of stories with you here on visualization.

In the mid 90's I was preparing to compete in one of the major events in Scotland. I had been out of solo competition in Scotland for about five years due to neck and back injuries, which led to spasms and an inability to control the instrument and my hands properly. Many years of all sorts of different physical therapies—chiropractic, massage, acupuncture, physiotherapy, heat and ice—have all helped to control both the pain and spasms. I combined this with going right back to basic scales and technical work as well. All of this work combined to retrain my hands with my mind and help get me back on my musical journey.

I was on the reserve list to play in the Gold Medal competition at the Argyllshire Gathering in Scotland, but when no one had withdrawn with just ten to twelve days to go, I had resigned myself to the fact that I would be playing in the silver medal (one level lower and an entirely different four tunes to carry in my repertoire) for that year.

During lunch on the day before, I received a call from the organizer telling me that I indeed had a spot due to a late cancellation and would be fourth or fifth on in the morning. My coach at the time was Bill Livingstone and he had no problem at all spending the afternoon with me to try to re-sync all of Gold Medal music back into my head. I was in good playing form and felt after a good solid afternoon of help that I was ready for the next day.

I arrived at the new venue with plenty of time and got myself prepared to play. All things seemed to be just fine until I walked out onto the floor to perform. This performance was a pure disaster. I should have stopped but I couldn't. My instrument was failing me (I thought) and this caused the musical performance to sink to a terrible low. I really just wanted to find the fastest way to hide or just get on a plane to come home.

What happened? I asked myself. And how did I not stop or fix the issue? Well, I was actually envisioning, but also thinking through like a competitor. I knew that this was my chance, the one I had asked for. But during the performance, I only had a small idea of what I was doing wrong. In my head I was saying over and over, "That has to be the last slip, calm down." I remember knowing full well that I was out of the prizes early on, but my own don't-quit instinct was there. I was thinking I could just play really well at the end, and at least the judges might think it was some unfortunate mechanical failure that caused this and still realize I was a good enough musician to get in the event next year once again. In yet another golf analogy, I think I was trying to save the round by making three birdies on 16,17,18.

Once I had finished playing, I knew right away that I was done. I was angry, very embarrassed, and confused. It took a long time to get over that performance, as it was also the season ending event. I realized that while I thought I had been "envisioning" this performance in a way to bring out good music, I was really only thinking about some notes. I was unfocused on the music and I let all the possible demons get in there to harm my musical path. I knew there would be good players there and I got scared all of a sudden trying to figure out how I could play in that event. This was one of the most terrible days in my musical career, but the start of a great learning lesson for me.

Another story: Fast forward to the next year, in spring, and thanks again to Bill Livingstone and some early success at the local winter competitions, I was invited to play at the prestigious Dr. Dan Reid Invitational in San Francisco. Once again, the preparation seemed to go very well. But it was not all that long since I had played at Oban the year prior, so I thought, Let's, go, I'm ready and I feel better than last year. I had been to Bill's house regularly for help going through the music and everything seemed to be fine.

When I arrived in San Francisco, I was greeted by a man named Ozzie Reid. Ozzie was the organizer of the Dr. Dan Reid Memorial. Ozzie took tremendous pride in this event and he wanted it to be known as the best and most challenging event there was for top pipers anywhere in the world. He was good friends with Bill, and by chance had met my father once or twice many years before. Ozzie felt it was fun to put immense pressure on people to add to the event itself.

As I arrived, he greeted Lillian (Bill's wife) with flowers, shook hands with Bill, and then as their luggage showed just before mine, blurted out (for the first of several times), "Right, Gandy. You ready, yet?" as if I had any power to sway a baggage handler. Then he called me by name as we neared the hotel, except he called me Ray (my deceased father's name) and that angered me. I finally just cheekily said back to him, "Ozzie, my friends call me Bruce." That was all I had. I didn't know if he was trying to put me over the edge or was just being rather hostile, but I was not in a very good mood. (By the way, this is all quite important for the event itself.)

When we arrived at the beautiful St. Francis Hotel and got to our rooms, there was a nice envelope full of things to do: some restaurant coupons, maps, and our confirmation to play and our tune lists. Well, my tune list was not correct! I knew this because I had a copy of my own entry with me. I called down to Ozzie's room and he said no, that's the list, he couldn't change it now. I proceeded to explain that this tune list was in fact Bill's list, because I had sent both of our tune entry lists in the same envelope as a favour to Bill since he was in a trial at the time.

Ozzie was still having none of this, almost calling me a liar as opposed to admitting that it was possible that his team had made an error. I was now furious and told him he had thirty minutes to make the change or I was going to just take a taxi to the airport and go back home. I was fed up with the disrespect, the back-handed remarks, and insult after insult.

I decided to stay after Ozzie allowed my list to be accepted, still not admitting fault but making it seem like he would bend the rules for me. We all had a good practice later on and a few of the competitors settled me down and let me know of some of their experiences with Mr. Reid also.

The next day I was ready to go. I was third or fourth on to perform, and I had heard some great playing that morning. It was exciting to listen to the players perform in the grand ballroom.

Straight to the point, I went out for the first event, the classical music, and everything fell apart again. I was so rattled and in awe playing alongside five of the world's top players that I just crumbled once again. Now I *really* wanted to just go home.

I went to my room, changed into my shorts and T-shirt and went out for a walk. I don't remember at all what I even thought of, except that I had truly embarrassed myself there. I never did ask for a copy of that performance, as I was scared to hear it. I did figure out though that for whatever reason when I got up there to play my "sound" seemed to disappear on that floor.

This is something that happens in nice rooms. The sound travels away from you and gets sucked up by the carpet and you listen to your pipes to try to set them. I knew about that from previous experiences elsewhere, but couldn't seem to relate that back to myself, as I was consumed with fear at that moment. I was feeling that my pipes were not good enough for this group, that I was not playing well enough to keep up with these great players. Everything negative that I could think of was going through my head, sort of a reverse visualization.

It was awful.

But then something happened. You see, this event was actually called the Dr. Dan Reid Memorial recital. Yes, it was a competition, but it was also a *recital* first and foremost, and you were there to play for your audience, the true employers of each and every one of us. Mistakes might throw you out of the contest, but you had to maintain some form and play through to the end.

I ate a small bite of lunch, put the uniform back on, and prepared to make my way to the tuning room to warm up for the next event. This time, I think, my draw might have been last on. As I was walking down the hall to where the warm up rooms were located I could only think, What are you going to do? This could be the end of my career. I needed to get rid of that thought fast.

By chance, in the tuning room was a big mirror and I looked at it and saw myself there. What a sight. This was not a musician ready to play. The person in the mirror looked like someone heading to the gallows.

This next moment changed my life.

I looked at the person in the mirror and I was not very happy, and as crazy as it sounds, I began to have a conversation with him. First was a lecture: "What do you think you're doing? What a fool, why are you actually letting that happen?" Basically, I somehow started to become an angry coach to myself. A good kick in pants was what I needed to stop feeling sorry for myself.

I then started talking to that person and explain to them that I needed to remember that those pipes sounded great yesterday in practice, there was nothing wrong with them. I called him by his name and said, "Bruce, you've beat Bill twice this year. You've been playing really great this year, and you got invited for that very reason. You are better than that garbage you pulled this morning. Why are you worried? If you play anything like you did in your practice session here, then that could easily set the standard, and those others will have to do something outstanding to beat you."

At that very moment I learned that if I am prepared and confident, with a good instrument, I am good enough to be one of those players, and I should *never try to WIN a contest.* Instead, I have always played and coached since that very day to *NEVER LOSE.* Don't give it away! Sure, someone may perform better. You can go back afterwards and iron out how they got past you. *But, if you are ready to play well and not lose yourself, you force the others to play at their very best.*

This is, honestly, a true story, as the results on the Internet would show. I went out there to perform, and the pipes were really fantastic right when I blew them up. I walked around the floor settling in, taking in the room, the well-mannered listeners, the adjudicators, and readied myself to play. I thought of as many obstacles and distractions as I could, and I stared at them and then thought, "No way. I'll show you how this should be."

This was possibly one of the best performances of my life, I'm sure 100 percent, because I had told myself to *just play like I can.* I was confident. I was there full of lung breath, not panting with nerves, and I really knew this was musical and I was laying it out there. I felt I had lost focus several times but didn't put a finger out of place. You see, I had not lost focus, I had actually gained a very weird inner focus, what some call an "out of body experience." I remember watching myself for parts of this and then coming back to myself on the floor again. It was all very surreal and kind of cool.

I played with a lot of heart and soul that day. When the desperation and worry started to creep back in, the hands were beginning to tighten on the grip. During the middle of the marching parts, I just said to myself, "Go to your kitchen," where I tended to do most of my practice. And it worked fantastically. I could see myself in my kitchen playing there, and I immediately began to relax. This is something that I still do to this day each time I am up on the platform or stage performing.

When I finished, I walked by Bill, who gave a small smile. I really didn't know if I had done all that well or not. What I did know was that it was better than the morning.

He came right into the tuning room to congratulate me. I'll never forget it when he said, "That was maybe the most remarkable recovery from a disaster that I have ever witnessed after what happened earlier." I sat down and told him the whole story about the walk into town, thinking, worrying, and then the part where I stood in front of a mirror and lectured that guy. He laughed, but just said the playing was just beautiful, and that he was familiar with this out-of-body experience. Many people get them, but most don't know they have had one or what was going on, just thinking they blanked out.

That day taught me about confidence and visualizing properly. I was not worried about Ozzie and his attitude towards me. In fact, I used that to power myself up with a quiet thought of "I'll show him." Keep in mind, this attitude is a *confident* "I'll Show Him" thought, *not* a cocky attitude, as that doesn't work that well either.

Incidentally, I won that second event that day, a very proud moment in life.

I continue to read up and practice visualization all of the time. When I am rehearsing in my music room, if things are going well, I then tell myself, often with the recorder on, that it's time to go onstage. *It takes concentration to trick your mind into believing you are somewhere else for more than a few seconds. But if you just keep at it, you can succeed.* It becomes a form of self-hypnosis. When I practice at home, I move to suddenly be on stage at any of several different venues, and, when I am on stage, nervous, I remind myself that the public wants to hear good music, and I use those words to myself: *Go to your kitchen!*

KEY TAKEAWAYS

❖ FEAR OF FAILURE: ARE YOU IN "FIGHT OR FLIGHT" MODE?

❖ HAVE YOU IMAGINED THE POSSIBILITIES? CAN YOU SEE THEM AND ANTICIPATE THEM?

❖ VISUALIZE EVERYTHING IN ADVANCE—PRETEND TO "BE THERE."

❖ USE A TRIGGER THOUGHT. "GO TO YOUR KITCHEN!" WHAT'S YOURS?

Your Personal Notes and Experiences

- What are your own reminders from this chapter?

....

....

....

....

....

....

....

....

....

....

....

....

....

....

....

....

....

For more information visit www.brucegandymusic.com

SECTION 3
Calm Your Nerves

*An ounce of practice is generally
worth more than a ton of theory.*

—E.F. Schumacher

Have you ever arrived at a venue and just felt that you forgot something? Perhaps a strange feeling of being lost is going on in your head? Stomach twitching? Maybe you are having a hard time being organized in your head? I have had all of these issues, many times over. They are simply known as nervous reactions.

You arrive at the park, or stage, or the course, and while you are thinking perhaps about the first step, your head is rushing to the next place. You may be informing the host or organizer that you have arrived, but it becomes hard to listen to their instructions because your emotional head is thinking about the performance. You brain feels like it's going at one hundred miles per hour since you left your home, and the lack of control over everything is just making you feel much worse. You want to perform, but right now, at this very moment in time, you are not sure that you are ready. Something has drastically changed since you left that safe zone called home. In fact, everything has changed and the idea of running away from it all or just not doing the event is winning over. But you came here to PLAY! You have practiced hard (or have you?). Rehearsals have been good and productive so far (or at least that's what you thought). The session with the coach was also very good (at least, that's what you remember).

So, what's going on?

Anticipation can create a great load of anxiety within your head and standing around and doing nothing, which should be relaxing, is often the complete opposite. We need to stretch, or take a few swings, or in my case, get the instrument out for three or four minutes to hear that it sounds good for the performance. This reassures that we didn't forget one of the many parts associated with rehearsing at home. We can then check one box of worry off of the list.

But why are we so nervous? What is driving this intense fear to perform and how can we stop it?

Let's start by looking at nerves themselves. (I am certainly not a doctor, so this is not clinical research. These stories come from years of study, asking questions, and analyzing people in their performance habits.) Nervousness can come from a variety of areas in your mind, but a few common triggers of nervous reactions or fears come from: expectation; fear of the unknown; fear of failure; lack of focus (often due to points two and three), in addition to other factors or pressures that you have placed upon yourself.

If you have studied and practiced the chapter on visualization, it can be a great help when you're at the performance level. When you are feeling on edge, you need to work to mentally transport yourself back to the driving range or the practice field or your downstairs studio where you are able to forget the world and anxiety and just play.

Many factors may or may not contribute to you feeling the pressure of that day, but trying to make a special day feel like any regular day means you should try to take all these added bumps in the road out of play and write a list of reminders down for yourself. Many of the items on my list here may seem obvious (and perhaps you execute them already, but if just one item helps you, then it's worth it). Remember, having extra pressures can take away any enjoyment of the performance itself, which will continue to spiral down to mediocrity or worse.

Here is a good portion of the list that I keep handy to focus and serve as a reminder:

1. **Preparation:** Whether it's music or sport, you should know weeks in advance the music which you intend to perform. You just cannot perform well if only the bare minimum has been done to prepare. This would be like buying new shoes from the store,

going for a walk in them, and thinking you can do a marathon the next day.

You may have all of the best and real reasons for not preparing, whether it is homework or extra shifts at work or family issues. All of those are good reasons and they justify, for you, why it may not go so well. It is then up to you to look deep inside and think all about hope versus expectation and be realistic. If you're not expecting to be perfect, at least being relaxed about it may help you perform to a higher standard.

2. **Know the venue**: Have you ever arrived at a competition field and began to fill your mind with worry? Possibly you're actually starting to become quite anxious. But then, weeks later or even the next year, you return to the same venue and it's much easier. You are now familiar with the driving route and you know how long it takes to arrive. You may also know where the parking area is in relation to the performance areas. The whole trip to this venue just becomes easier and helps to put you at ease for the day, as you are going to the familiar surroundings.

   If you are going to a new place, you should plan to arrive good and early. This gives you time to relax, stretch, or walk around and take some of it in, as opposed to rushing to the first tee or perhaps the performance platform without any or very little warm-up at all.

3. **Understand the event:** The adjudicators and especially the audience want you to do well. *So many people worry that this one or that one will not like their performance that they fall to pieces worrying, spending all their time thinking that they are not good enough.*

   Try to think about the performance from the adjudicator's or audience's point of view. A judge may be watching or listening to ten or twenty or more performances. If everyone is performing poorly, that is not a very enjoyable day for the adjudicator, so of course they are eager for you to perform well. If you are performing a recital hall, then the audience has come to support you. They've taken time from their busy schedules and often paid good money to watch or listen to you, so of course they're hoping that you and/or your team do well.

4. **Sleep well the night before:** This should go without saying, but it bears reminding. If you can be relaxed the night before an event and get a good sleep, not only will your body feel more rested, but science tells you that you will feel better for it. Get a good night's rest before performance and you will feel much more vibrant and focused the next day.

5. **Exercise and eat well:** Once again, stating what may sound obvious, but is not often followed. This is even more true on performance day. Trying to eat good food at a venue can be a challenge as you may be at the mercy of the vendors. For those long days, energy bars and especially bananas (my personal favourite) can help to save you and keep you going, instead of some greasy fried food from a vendor. If you are doing a music show or competition where you will stand in place for a while, try to get some brisk walking in to keep the blood flowing whenever you get a chance.

6. **Develop and rely on a routine:** Do this for these events and stick to it. If you are used to getting up early and doing some sort of activity each morning before your coffees and emails and web surfing, then try to follow that on performance day. Yes, it can be tough if you have to travel and rise up early to do so, but planning even the ten-minute stretching session and having food ready the night before can help. If you have a routine that you go through at home before your run through, leave yourself time to warm up that way on performance day. When you create a habit of the procedure, then the routine stays in place and you're able to put

your energies and a clear mind into the delivery of the performance itself.

When I travel with my band to the world bagpipe championships, it never seems too difficult to get everyone up and ready for practice by 9 a.m. sharp. We do this for a variety of reasons. The main reason is that we know we will be performing in the early morning on the competition day itself, so we try to acclimatize our bodies and our instruments to the weather. The potential jet lag is still present and we need to become used to performing at that time of the day.

The same should hold true for a person performing very late in the evening. When people work a night shift on their jobs they have to realign the days to fit in the normal daytime activities but still get enough sleep to allow them to be fresh and sharp at night.

The whole idea is to not create a shock to your system. If you were playing a concert show and performing at p.m., you might want to rehearse at that time of night if it is possible.

I used to feel that I was not a morning person. I guess I still do in some ways. But I have come to read and believe that this is more a state of mind. At the time of writing much of this book I've been working on a new routine to be more productive. I wake up at 5:30, grab a large water bottle, and work out for twenty to thirty minutes. This gets the heart rate up and releases all sorts of good chemicals into the body, which makes me much sharper. Then I come to the table and write for a while on this book or in a personal journal.

If someone was to tell me a year ago that I would be writing, editing, and personal journaling at 6 a.m., I would've laughed. Now I look forward to this peaceful time each day, as the workout routine combined with the silence of the early morning allows me to think clearly to accomplish some of the tasks I want to do that day.

While this is not about getting up early and accomplishing your tasks early, it does relate to the fact that when you start to create a routine you can create a habit you can perform more confidently, whether it's playing golf, playing an instrument, or waking up for a workout first thing in the morning. Newer studies show that it takes sixty-six days to develop a habit or routine, so don't give up on yourself.

7. **Record yourself at home:** This was covered previously but certainly falls into the area of calming your nerves as well. It is good to record yourself at times to get the audio and visual feedback so you can track your progress. You can also record yourself, again using either audio or video, just to get used to that machine and pretend that it's your adjudicator or the audience watching you.

   Remember, the more proficient you become with this technique, the greater your focus will be. Set up the audio or video recorder as often as possible when you're on the real stage or playing field. With this, you will gain real perspective and evidence on how you performed live, as opposed to how you thought it actually was.

8. **One-eighty Factor:** This very important technique really follows you throughout the entire journey. From an initial practice, to the rehearsal stage, to the live performance and even moving forward, keep your own One-eighty Factor paper with you.

   It is always easy to come up with the difficulties and the obstacles which make you feel as though you can't do something and these issues can wind you up into a nervous frenzy. When I coach musicians, from young kids to adults and even seniors, I try not to allow the word "cannot" to enter into the Clubhouse studio. If you can spend just a couple minutes actually writing down these issues, you will very quickly discover many of the solutions to the issues.

You can also use this notepad to refresh your memory when working with your coach. Ask yourself why you feel these little problems are occurring without laying blame on some other person, circumstance, or venue. That is the start to solving some of these issues.

Many people use this basic practice several times a day in their lives for many different items by recognizing the problem, answering in their head what would make it better, and finally writing down what needs to be done to accomplish this.

Remember, writing on a note pad by hand and actually writing and reading the statement brings a deeper commitment to that resolution. If you can mentally solve most of the potential issues, you'll be much calmer when you need to be.

9. **Breathe:** One final tip to help combat nerves is using some form of breathing exercise. Once again, I'm not a doctor or a therapist, so I will not give any real medical advice on the different techniques. Suffice to say, the number of people I see who are in a near-panic mode before they perform is frightening. Do some research, find out or ask about one or more methods of deep breathing that might work for you and practice this technique. Then remind yourself at times to take a few minutes to breathe and settle your body's natural rhythm.

Many times when I have been at the competition venue with my students, I have used this technique myself or while coaching one of my musicians. Take some deep breaths together and begin to focus on the breath yourself. After a few breaths I ask them to slow the intake of air so that they slowly breathe in for a longer count and then they exhale long and slowly.

A great tip for this type of breathing it is to count slowly when you are inhaling a breath in. For the tougher exhale, try to make a humming sound from your mouth as you exhale the air. This helps to keep the flow of air steady, if the humming sound from your mouth is consistent. When the sound gets higher pitched or even louder then you know you're exhaling the air at the different rate of consistency.

Using long, deep breaths makes it easier to concentrate as you're focusing on the number of breaths and the sound of them, seeking equal breaths all the way in and out. The better you settle into this and think through your own breath, the more likely this will help to relax you immensely.

KEEP THIS LIST HANDY
FOR CONTROLLING NERVES

1. Preparation

2. Know the venue

3. Understand the event

4. Sleep

5. Exercise and eat well

6. Develop and rely on a routine

7. Record yourself at home

8. Use the One-eighty Factor to address variables

9. Breathe

SECTION 4
Aiming for Brilliance

Perfection is not attainable,
but if we chase perfection we can catch excellence.
—*Vince Lombardi*

When you are about to take the stage, you realize what an incredible challenge you are about to embark on. You have put hours and weeks into your practice, preparation, and rehearsal, and by this time you feel ready. But something both magical and frightening can happen at the venue. What you expect should happen, or how you expect anything to happen, can change quickly and put all your hopes into a free fall.

Most of my students have high hopes of success, because we train very hard and rehearse as much as possible to have the required elements ready. Or at least that's what I hope to see in everyone. But it's not always like that, as you will see in the next story.

With a big competition coming up in the United States, I offered my house for a full day of guidance and instruction to seven local players who were going to be travelling to this event. What I thought was going to be a fun day for me and the players to get a few coaching tips turned out to be a tremendous learning experiences on the view of hopes versus expectations.

We changed up four things from the regular practice that these people were used to doing at home. This was not done to make this a challenge. It was actually done to make this day more of a master class situation and a fun run through of what might happen on the real day. These four differences were: one, I had a recording unit set up on a tripod to record the performances; two, I also had my pad of paper in front of me to write down notes as the performer played (in my world of competitive bagpiping we are used to seeing the adjudicators with the pads of paper, so I wanted to simulate a competitive event); three, I invited all of the players to stay for the whole day to watch and maybe pick up some other tips (there were six or seven people listening each time one of the performers was playing); and four, we had the music that they were to perform.

These were all well accomplished musicians here, not beginners, on this particular day. In the classical bagpipe events and in these upper levels of competitive performance the performers have to submit three, sometimes four pieces of music, with one piece selected, the name of which is usually shown to the player in the final room before they go on to play. This only gives the player fifteen minutes or so to do a final rehearsal on their piece. I gave them an hour on this day. I was trying to make it slightly similar to a contest setting, and expected them to know them by now and be ready for this.

So, I felt this was a good idea: everyone together, hearing each other, cheering each other on, and maybe learning a few things from the dialogue and tips I was giving to each of them.

While they thought they had things going well and were hoping they would play well, their expectations were that they were ready and warmed up and this should be fine. Rehearsal at their homes the day before, or two days before, were positive, but when we changed up the atmosphere by adding these four new components it very much rattled all but one of the players.

I spoke to them about being the player that they are, and that they were better than this, while trying not to be too negative about the fact that, all things considered, the music was not really going very well this day and it was just over two weeks until the event.

This realization shocked the players, and was a terrific learning experience. The value was immense. These players felt as if they were in the recording studio when it wasn't that at all. This was just set up to record their own practice session for them to listen to and gain helpful feedback. I was not going to send this out to other people; I wasn't keeping a recording myself. As for taking notes, when you're performing, and you see people writing, often this makes you fear that they are criticizing you, when actually I may have been writing as a reminder to both of us that part A or B or whatever in their selection was really quite nice. I was enjoying some particular part, or the tone of their instrument was very good at this point and holding well. But when a performer sees the person writing they may go into a panic mode thinking they are doing something wrong, instead of being confident enough in their own performance.

When you bring the same set of skills from one venue into a new place and do not familiarize yourself with potential hazards (like the recording device or the crowd), then if something is not absolutely perfect, you can go into panic mode, the performance falls apart and you lose all hope. Using the One-eighty Factor, we need to ask ourselves: "What could go wrong?" and "How might this situation actually *be*?" We can then think of the good result we'd like to achieve and write down our action items to ensure the proper result.

For instance, if you have to perform outside and it's very cold in the morning, don't just show up and be cold. You need to think how you are going to combat that. You need to dress warmly, make sure you have some hot drinks with you, have mittens. For us pipers, it goes even deeper: we need to understand how long to play and warm up, so when you do hit the outside, you're still able to perform at some level. It may not be as refined or polished as what you can do inside, but you can get rid of some of the elements that contribute to some disasters.

That's a very easy, and rather obvious example of the One-eighty Factor. On this particular day, the students could have taken several of these "issues" they encountered at this time and made their lives a lot easier for themselves by taking just a few moments to understand this new environment.

Look at the first element: They are going to perform in front of a group of their peers. Instead of being worried that they will look silly in front of them or they won't be "good enough" or that they might be embarrassed that they are going to make a mistake, they need to remember that these other performers are in the same boat. They're cheering hard on the inside for them. They want them to do well. The performer should not be frightened of this situation. The players should embrace the smiles and the encouragement coming through in the moment.

The second element is the recording machine that they are staring at with that bright red *record button* on. First, the person gets up, sets their instrument up in tune correctly, and takes a nice deep breath. The performer needs to feel at that moment that she can do this, and not be trying to do something more than she has done previously. She needs to keep the focus, to see the music in her mind's eye to help concentrate on the act itself. When you see that red light as a threat, you start to question everything. Once you do that, you are inviting disaster.

If you are a golfer or have watched golf, how many times have you hit good shots on the driving range, only to go out on the course and hit the ball right into the lake? It was an easy shot, the lake may not even be in your way, but once you lose your commitment due to worrying about *not* hitting it in the lake, your unconscious helps you to steer the ball right there. In golf, you lose a ball, take a penalty stroke and you move on, and have a chance to get that stroke back.

But in music, we get it in our heads that there is this "permanent record" of the performance. (Remember, we are still talking here about a rehearsal performance, not a live show.) Remind yourself that if things go downhill, all you need to do is regroup and do it again, and erase the previous attempt and it's gone.

I'm a big fan of working both ends of this recording. I want the performer to relax and really understand that while their playing is important, it can still be erased to avoid feeling bad or embarrassed. On the other hand, in setting an exact time to play and putting a little pressure on the situation much like this, you try to envision the real event in your mind, and when you get worked up, you use this situation to anticipate the nerves you will have at the "real event." You use the One-eighty Factor to ask the questions to help figure out the differences between playing here and playing at home: At home you are confident because you rehearse in your own studio, you put the work in, you know the piece you have been working on, and nobody is questioning your ability. When you arrive at the next venue you expect to make it perfect. This is where the recording tool, used at home in practice and rehearsal, can help you anticipate and eliminate those additional distractions and pressures to perform on the day.

The third element is just to remember that the person (or coach) is writing notes to help you, not scold you. It can be easier for the coach to jot down notes as you are performing, as this lets you go through the entire selection and then have it reviewed. If you are worrying about what the judge may write, that sends a message that you have no confidence in what you have rehearsed. Flipping that around in the One-eighty Factor, remind yourself that you are ready to perform, that this performance is going to be really good, and that the judge's writing is all about the positive aspects of the playing. Once you are done, then you can read the notes and discuss the performance. *You should be trying to enjoy the positives and, instead of reading the comments as "points off," read them as just notes informing you why this part was not quite as good as the other part.*

Here is another good segue back to golf. If you've ever listened to a pro talk after a modest or not so great round, they rarely say, "I played awful today." More often than not they will say, "I hit a lot of good shots out there and easily could have had a good round going. Unfortunately, I missed those shots on this hole and that hole, which made it tough to get a good score on that hole." They see the good in their game, and it gives them a positive feeling for how to go out and tidy up the parts that were perhaps not wrong, but just not as good as they could have been.

Finally, there's the music that has been selected. It's just human nature often to have "your pick or your choice" that you would like to play. With four pieces there for selection, the chance of you getting what the listener wants to hear is 25 percent. That's not very good odds at all. This can be disastrous, and this happened a couple of times on that day. People are meant to be very close-to-ready for this event, but some players only know one or two of their pieces really well. Other selections are coming along but are not really performance-ready. So, what happens when by chance the selection that I have asked for on the day is not the one you have been putting most of the work into? These people have played Russian roulette here, and knowing that they are not quite there most likely means that the performance itself will clearly show that they are not yet fully prepared to perform at the level that is expected of them. This was certainly the case on this day for those performers.

In this way, yes, what I did was a test of sorts. I had asked everyone to have their selections ready. It is a difficult task to complete, but they must come in ready and confident to have a good chance at performing successfully. No matter which of the four selections is asked for, they must be thinking, Great, I know I can really entertain you with this one, and come into the studio ready to pour their musical hearts and souls out on the floor.

KEY TAKEAWAYS

❖ CALM YOUR NERVES. BE PREPARED, AND INNER GREATNESS CAN OVERPOWER ANXIETY!

❖ REALITY CHECK—GET OVER YOURSELF! THE AUDIENCE AND ADJUDICATORS ARE EAGER FOR YOU TO PERFORM WELL.

❖ DON'T RUN ON FUMES. EAT AND STAY HYDRATED.

❖ THE PLAYBOOK. ARE YOU USING THE ONE-EIGHTY FACTOR TO STICK TO YOUR ROUTINE ON GAME DAY?

❖ TECHNOLOGY TODAY. HAVE YOU BEEN RECORDING TO GET A "LIVE" CHECK?

❖ THE WORLD WILL NOT END WITH TRYING. YOU CAN STILL ERASE IN A REHEARSAL ATTEMPT.

Your Personal Notes and Experiences

- What are your own reminders from this chapter?

....

....

....

....

....

....

....

....

....

....

....

....

....

....

....

....

....

....

....

For more information visit www.brucegandymusic.com

PART FOUR
Moving Forward

Bruce at the Donald MacDonald Quaich, Skye, Scotland 2015.

The work you have done up to now has focused a great deal on the mechanics of preparation. But as any expert in any field of performance will tell you, your art is more than the sum of the individual parts of practice/rehearse/perform. It is a *calling*.

There are other things you can do to help yourself improve, things that lie just outside the scope of your own practice regime. They all help you become a better musician by creating and taking advantage of opportunities to grow, learn, immerse, and develop. The Total Preparation Package has to include these areas, or else it wouldn't be "total."

In this chapter we will explore the ways in which you can grow by helping others, becoming a good leader, and becoming an inspiration to others. All of these contribute to your development as a more complete artist and performer.

SECTION 1
Help Your Friends

Individual shows, small-group games, and other performance options serve many purposes, and can be both rewarding *and* lonely. You have put days or perhaps weeks of effort into one performance. This may be part of a series of shows or a single tournament or year ending performance/recital. However, when it's over, you are done.

For many people wishing to advance themselves, the attention shifts to the *next* performance (right away). *You* may need to think this way at times, as you may be on a small tour in several cities or playing for several evenings, so you have to continue on the path to get the job done and pay your bills.

Personally, I feel that I am a bit of an adrenaline junkie and thrive on the process of getting ready for a competition more than the result. But I'd be lying if I said I wasn't concerned about the result or placing itself, and most people who are really trying hard to better themselves care about the result as well. Why is it so important? Quite simply (and this is my own view here), the results give you an answer to all of the work you have put in.

But whatever way you approach it, it can be a hard thing to go through: all the ups and downs, all the hard work practicing and preparing, all the feelings you may have after reading the results (maybe they weren't as good as you hoped, or maybe they were great, but that feeling doesn't last forever as the next performance has to be considered). *Having a friend or a group of people to help through all of this will help more than you can imagine.*

A FRIEND THROUGHOUT THE SEASON

I know a piper who takes lessons steadily, works very hard at her music, and tries very hard to overcome nerves and bad vibes, so much so that she has taken competition to a new level. She feels that with weekly help from her coach she can play and improve without dealing with the judging sheets, which can often read either negative or not tell you much at all. So, she has a friend who goes to each of her events with her, gives her encouragement and collects her score sheets and the medals for her. But only at the *end* of the season do they go through all of the judges' sheets, and *then* she decides how she did that season.

That is just one instance of a friend helping another to achieve a goal and help enjoy performing more without all the negative thoughts. In a competitive environment it may seem a bit extreme to wait until the end of the season to look at judges' sheets, and it took me a while to appreciate this, but I get it now. Instead of performing for one day and getting results and feedback, she performs for one full season and then condenses all of the feedback into a "very good" column and a "need to work on" column.

This cannot happen without help and support from a friend.

For myself, *I now feel that helping friends is a very important part of the musical circle of life.* I have been very fortunate to have had a lot of great results over my competitive career thus far. Sure, you feel good because you won, but the feeling does not last like it does when you help your friends to achieve a big goal in their own playing.

HELPING FORWARD

Some people say we should help others because it's good to "give back." I recently read *The Opportunity* by Eben Pagan (one of the growing breed of internet course developers and entrepreneurs) who states, "I don't do this to give back. It would imply that I took something to start." I whole-heartedly agree with that idea, and I worry that the phrase is used very loosely now. Yes, helping can be explained as "giving back," but it can also be described as *helping forward*.

Personally, I have been helped endlessly over the years, and I have acquired so much musical knowledge thanks to the openness and sharing from coaches and other great performers. I have been fortunate to hear and share time and ideas with many great people who I did not feel they "owed it" to society to "give back." They simply paid it forward, with no sense of obligation; it was more like they did it out of generosity. When you help anyone *forward* with anything at all (from holding a door open to explaining the most difficult musical passage over and over again), it comes from the heart.

Helping your musical friends to achieve a goal can occur in so many forms, and they all help the end result. You can help financially, physically, mentally, musically, and in many other ways. Take a look at the full picture and see where you fit in.

WAYS OF HELPING FORWARD

Financially. Think of a typical parent here. They pay for all of the lessons, the instrument parts, entry fees to events, and the list goes on. Some people do not have parents who can afford all of that. Maybe you can help them yourself, or help them find the financial resources through grants, fundraisers, or other money-earning opportunities. As a young person, I grew up in a family that would not be considered wealthy at all money-wise, but somehow, I still got to all of the events and never went hungry either. A lot of people around me made it financially possible to achieve my dreams, and I have never forgotten that to this day.

Physically. Think here of all the instrument parts that need replacing. These can be loaned or given or bought as needed so the musician moves forward. There can be several different types of uniform parts that are needed as well. Over time, items tend to either wear out or kids can outgrow them or the style or requirements may change. You may be able to help someone here by lending or giving an item that you have.

Physically helping could also be as simple as driving a person to and from a venue, such as team practice or an event.

I have lots of friends who just love to be a small part of the team, and they are willing to help out with the work that's needed to help make things happen, be it for an individual or a full team. Perhaps you volunteer to come to some of the musician's rehearsals and operate an audio recorder or video recorder to capture their playing, so the performer can review the rehearsal work later on. This could easily become a reciprocal agreement for you both to help each other, perhaps even at the same session. Offering to help by taking on a physical task means that the performer has one less task to do, which becomes one less distraction and frees up the mind to focus on the music, making it ready for a performance. This follows the same for sports.

I remember walking around a Canadian Professional Golf Association event and having an opportunity to speak with a young Mike Weir (2003 Masters Champion) during a break. I asked him how he managed being on the road, away from family, wife, and not really making enough money at that time. He was immediately very gracious to a car company for letting him rent certain types of cars at many of the tour stops.

He was also so grateful to the telephone company that had given him a cell phone to travel. It was preprogrammed with his wife's and his parents' number and he could call from anywhere in North America, anytime. This was a big thing at the time, as cell phones were not all that common back then. Breaking into the professional golf tour can be a very difficult and lonely struggle, and the importance of having the ability to call home to talk about the day kept Mike moving forward. What seems like perhaps a small gesture from a sponsor really turned out to be a huge help to Mike. Being able to talk through some of the loneliness or emotions of his playing to his partner or parents helped him to move forward. Mike went on to be a very successful golfer on the PGA with career winnings of over twenty-five million dollars, and this may not have happened without the help from his friend, the telephone company.

The same follows when you or your team have travelled a long distance to an unfamiliar place to perform or complete. Many extra hands helping with the multitude of extra tasks gets the job done quicker and easier. This allows the group more time to think about their performance, without worrying about the smaller tasks involved in getting there. Top groups or acts have this work down to a science. They employ a team of people to help them to organize their travel, schedule, meals, hotel, and all other chores.

I was witness to this a few years back when our band was asked to join Sir Paul McCartney on stage for a performance. In the case of Sir Paul McCartney, this is big business with a huge staff of people all over the field handling logistics of every sort. Although this was on a much bigger scale than anything our band had ever done, it showed us that if all the non-musical performance items were covered by an effective team of people, the show not only ran more smoothly, but Sir Paul could be very relaxed. We saw him leaving his private room and being led to the stage by his assistant—his one and only focus was to play music without distraction.

During the time our group had prepared in the weeks and days leading up to the concert, we really had no idea of how this was all going to work once we arrived at the event. Where were we supposed to go? Front, back, secret side entrance, street entrance? We had no idea. But once we were within a week of the scheduled show, their organizer called and told us exactly where to go and what time to be there. "We'd like you here for sound check at 3 p.m., where we will bring you all to a large room where you can then warm up. Sir Paul has the run-through on this song scheduled for 4:15 p.m., and we will come and get you and bring you to the stage." *All of the worries about the small incidentals were now gone and this gave us the ability to fully focus on the performance.* This freedom to concentrate on our performance elevated our playing, and the group became much more solid at the sound check and even better for the show that evening.

What these pros do is itemize every detail that goes into a show, right down to having a bottle of water on the stage for the artist. They check them off one by one, so that the artist only thinks about the music.

I have learned now that no detail is too small. So, if you now find that you are in a position to help a friend on a small task, it will help largely in the end for the performer.

Mentally. Stage fright and fear of the unknown are very difficult obstacles to overcome for a performer. Lack of confidence and a wanting to rehearse "just one more time" generally creates a lot of uncertainty in the mind of the performer. As a coach or friend, my job is not only to teach the person to do x, y, z over and over, but to understand what they are currently capable of and what may be worrying them. A friend or coach must be able to read the person to some extent and help them overcome their fears. You cannot just say, "Don't worry, it's not hard really. You're just worried." That is not going to help. You need to dig deep and try to find out what's really going on there and unlock the trigger.

I had a wonderful experience with a young person back in August of 2017 while coaching a band preparing for the World Pipe Band Championships. This young lady was to perform in one of the two events. She was struggling with a mechanical part of the instrument, and this was affecting her ability to blow the tone and perform musically to the standard needed.

When the band finished rehearsing Set 1, she and two other players worked separately on their own beside the group. I went over with a big positive smile and said, "All right, are you ready?" Two of them bounced up, throwing high fives and screaming, "Yeah, you know it!" They were pumped!

I turned to the third and asked, and I could see terror on her face. She had a wee issue with a drone causing some problems with her strike-in. She burst into tears. This poor girl knew this music and wanted to play so very badly, but didn't get all the mechanics together. She feared that now trying on her own she was caught and would be cut. I told her the opposite! "Now that I can see and hear what's going on, we can fix this!" This only took about five minutes and I used the time to remind her that she had worked hard and spent hours around the table with the group, and we would not let "a faulty spark plug" stop her from performing. She trusted my experience and the knowledge that I brought in to help with these types of situations.

Very soon, we had the instrument ready and I said, "Try it!" She struck in and it was fine and sounding pleasant. But she was still tentative and just didn't think it would work. Test number two: I said, "Just do it again, but this time try to see yourself in the circle and just play." It worked! The band had just been dismissed, so I said calmly and quietly, "Let's do five starts in the medley, just the start for about thirty seconds." She nailed it every time. A big smile lit up her face with tears in her eyes saying, "Thank you, I really believe I will get to play tomorrow."

A big huge hug came after their performance, so many "thank you"s and "Please, please can we have a picture. You have helped so much this week for me to find out that I can do more and learn to believe it."

I didn't play. All I did was help out with some mechanics and encouragement for her to believe that she could also deliver her own awesome. It was truly one of the greatest mentoring moments in my life. It has been a long time since I have had the opportunity to help turn a band around under pressure, and seeing them get a prize I was screaming with joy and had to run into the area where all the bands were to find them to congratulate them. That alone was easily the highlight of my trip, and really shows where helping someone can make your heart swell with pride and happiness!

Tuning a band before World Championship final 2015.

Musically. Over many years of coaching and observing other people offering advice, I have learned a few important things. One must know all of what is needed before offering, as you can do damage when you "think" you're just saying this or that.

If you think you have a suggestion and you are prepared to give it, then it all depends on the Five W's:

Who are you offering advice to? Should you be offering them advice? Are you offering or telling them that they're wrong in their performing or in their approach to the performance itself? Be careful that what you are saying is fair to help the person, not show off your superiority.

What are you telling them? Will they understand this, or just become more confused? If you are offering advice, make sure the person understands. Don't just tell them: explain it!

When/Where. You are helping out a group to get ready, young kids perhaps, and you see someone and hear them poorly executing a certain passage. You know you can help. But you must remember that saying something that you may think is helping can also hurt the person's confidence, particularly if you tell them in the circle in front of others. Depending on the person or group, you may find it much wiser to wait for an appropriate time to offer this advice, or simply pull the person out of the group, off to the side, and fix the issue quietly without embarrassment.

Why. Quite simply, if you are in a position to help someone or a group and they recognize that your skills and experience can mutually benefit the project, then as an artist, why not?

Let me tell you a true story of a time I asked for help: I had composed a piece of music several years ago to honour a great lady who ran a music association I was involved with for a long time. This piece was in the form of our classical music, *piobaireachd*.

When I arrived at Northern Meeting Piping Competition at Inverness, Scotland, I saw Allan MacDonald of Glen Uig. Allan is one of three very famous piping brothers, and also a scholar in Gaelic history and song, as well as an authority on our classical music. Some years back Allan wrote a thesis on the relationship between Gaelic song and piobaireachd. So, I thought, who better to listen to my new piece and give me the seal of approval than this highly educated music scholar, and player whom I had great admiration for? Folks at home liked it, but if Allan did, I thought that I would have a winner.

I asked him for a couple minutes of time, to which he obliged, and I began to sing through the piece. When I finished there was an uncomfortable pause, which turned into Allan telling me, "Och, that's just a pile of notes that fits into the right key. There's not really much substance to it, and I don't know what you're trying to convey with the song."

Wow—that was like a large foot kicking me squarely and I said, "Oh okay, I'll need to look at this again." I was seriously hurt with a broken ego, but began to think about it and wonder, What's really wrong with this? Everyone else loved it, so I take it to the man who is so well versed in this style and he slammed it. I thought, I need to find out what's wrong or why this feels so bad for him, when others enjoyed it. I'm not so sure I was looking for praise, but more a seal of approval that the little Canadian boy could compose something with a true Gaelic feel.

I approached Allan once again and this is the conversation:

Me: "Allan, I'm a bit confused here."

Allan: "Why?"(He acted as if he did not recall any of the conversation fifteen minutes prior.)

Me: "I played this and most people took a liking to it, but you came out and just said it's crap, a pile of garbage, no meaning at all."

Allan: "Well, yes, I guess I did. But what does that matter?"

Me: "You're a man that I respect as a player, composer, etc., and respect your opinion, that's why."

Allan: "Bruce, you've composed three or four books of music. Your music has been played by soloists, pipe bands, and folk bands around the world. Who am I to tell you anything about your compositions? It is not my place to say it's either great or terrible. It's your place to decide, and more so, your audience when you perform the piece."

Me: "Ok, I take your point and thank you, but doesn't that seem just a wee bit harsh."

Allan: "Oh aye, *but I felt you could take it* and would ask if you had a difference in thought. Again, *who am I to tell you what you can or cannot play?* That is one of the big problems in piping just now. Too many people that know bugger all placing barriers and constraints on what we can and cannot play."

This probably sounds rather harsh, but because of his explanation I accepted it as a valuable learning lesson.

If you play your music, that's fine. It may be great or not so much, but if other people play it and it stands the test of time, then no one person can tell you otherwise.

Allan was just trying to help, maybe in a bit of the "school of hard knocks" style, but he was *teaching me to believe*. I get his point, but to this day I still run all of new music past a couple of trusted people I know who always "help a friend" by answering and screening all of the tunes that I send.

Helping a friend is an important piece of the overall package you carry as a musician.

KEY TAKEAWAYS

❖ HELPING OTHERS. ARE YOU "HELPING FORWARD"? THERE IS A SENSE OF POSITIVITY IN DOING THIS *VERSUS* GIVING BACK (THAT COMES WITH A SENSE OF "OWING").

❖ DOING A FAVOUR. ONE SMALL GESTURE CAN HAVE A HUGE IMPACT ON ANOTHER PERSON.

❖ LISTEN TO THE PERSON. HELP THAT PERSON UNLOCK THEIR "WORRY TRIGGERS."

❖ ASK FIRST! KNOW THE FIVE W'S OF THE STATEMENT BEFORE OFFERING UP SUGGESTIONS.

Your Personal Notes and Experiences

- What are your own reminders from this chapter?

....

....

....

....

....

....

....

....

....

....

....

....

....

....

....

....

....

....

For more information visit www.brucegandymusic.com

SECTION 2
Learn to Lead

As we move forward on our performing journey through life, we hit many roadblocks along the way. One such roadblock occurs when a person becomes what might be described as "stale." The performer has spent years on the first three parts of the journey and has hit a roadblock.

Developing a real routine can be terrific when applied to specific tasks in life and/or music and sport when a routine just "has to be done." For example, each morning I wake up, drink water, and then do some form of exercise, usually downstairs in my studio room (known as "the Clubhouse").I do this because I know it is good for me and allows me to pursue many of the other things in life that I enjoy by maintaining good health.

But I also know that the fastest and easiest way to fall out of a routine is to become bored or stale with the process. The answer seems simple. We must commit to and follow our morning routine, but we also need to change it up frequently so that the activity feels fresh and exciting. One day could be stretching or yoga, the next day possibly running or a different workout.

Transfer this thought pattern to your own music and you can see where this is leading. This book has four main components for a reason. If we spend each year or each season or each tour doing the same three items it can leave a person wanting for more.

1. We get music and we practice the scores to get the notes and arrangement to be part of the memory. It's always exciting at first to get new music to work on.

2. We then rehearse the music, sometimes on our own, other times with a group, as we try to concentrate and develop confidence in our raw ability to play. This allows us to start to think about the

pure feel of the music. Hopefully, this starts to become both fun and accomplished, as we now begin to anticipate and envision the live performance.

3. We are now performing at the local recital, or competition, or a bigger venue (more pressure), or a tour of any size. We learned the music, we have rehearsed all the scores, and now we are on stage. Now we try to keep nerves calm while feeling out our audience and delivering world best performance with all the confidence and passion we can let out. We are now delivering music to our true employer, the audience, and it's no longer about "being in the moment" as much as it is about giving our friends, coach, audience, or judges the best musical experience possible. That is what it's all about.

But then it ends. The recital or concert or tournament is over now and we go back to square one. This may be okay for a lot of people, and the three-stage process of Practice, Rehearse, Perform can be enough to keep them going year after year.

But like we mentioned in the previous section, there is another step: helping people forward. That not only serves a great cause in helping people, but it can also benefit your own ability tremendously, if you use the knowledge that you have gained and begin to *learn to lead*.

Similar to helping your friends, which makes you feel good, learning to lead develops other players' abilities and helps develop your own personal skill set and confidence at the same time.

Leading is not about being the boss and telling people off. It's more about guiding them along on their current path, be it with music or sport. There are times, however, in a team or band environment, where the leader occasionally has to engage the people in the group in a "boss-like" manner to get them to focus, or attend rehearsal, or learn their part of the score so they are not letting the team down. But the leader must pick and choose those battles appropriately. So, if that time comes, this potentially harsh message from the leader gets delivered with a sting-like effect. Whether it is emotionally raising the voice, or sending a message to the group about how they are disappointing everyone by not collectively pulling their weight, nobody wants harsh feedback all the time. That just doesn't help. *So, pick the time carefully to exercise this method.*

Much more importantly, the true leader is the person that can guide or coach a person or team to a much higher level than where they started. A good leader will use all off their available resources, including other people, to elevate the level of performance to new highs each time. As you gain days, weeks, or years of experience, you start to learn how to tap into each individual's mind and heart to get the very best out of them.

In music people can display a higher sense in one or more of the disciplines required for a performance. Taking a bagpipe group performance as an example, many parts go together to make the wheel turn:

We have people that sight read quickly.

We have people with good, clean, accurate hands.

We have people that seem good with the memory parts.

We have people with good stamina, but not a great ear for the tone.

We have people that blow a lovely, harmonic sounding instrument (not that skirling sound or killing-the-cat sound that has made bagpiping a bit of a joke for many years).

Not long ago I had the great challenge and personal experience to be brought in by a band to coach and lead the group for five days to help prepare them for the World Pipe Band Championship. I was fortunate in that the morning I arrived, the band had a scheduled performance already lined up in town. This gave me a chance to just begin in a small way to help with tuning, but more importantly, it gave me the chance to observe the group as a whole in their performance mode. I could see how the leader was able to deal with the details of the show and inform the group at appropriate times. This show had the band playing in two spots on one of the main streets in the city. Both of these were within walking distance and then the group moved to a third and final spot at a main park. The leader of the group had to plan out which music would be played at different spots and make sure everyone knew the running order of the sets. The job of all the other musicians in the band was to stay in control, and with all of the distractions around, keep focused on the task at hand.

I watched as the group performed their music, and this gave me a chance to see the body language from some of them. This alone can give you a sense of the players and is a really good start later on when coaching. Some players look calm and comfortable with their instrument. Others seem deep in focus, while other members look perhaps in near panic (as if they do not know a particular score well enough).Still others may be struggling with their instrument in some way, which makes the performance more challenging.

In between the sets, while walking from venue A to B, I got a chance to talk with many of them. In this group there were young high school students, younger professionals, new parents, and middle-aged folks making up the ensemble. In years of doing workshops and master classes, you become somewhat skilled at gauging folks. You realize that you cannot just lead everyone in the group the same way to get the most out of them. You find all sorts of personalities in a group that you learn to coach.

In very general terms, there are always a few that are confident and very skilled—it's always great to have a couple of folks like this so we can spread them around the circle. They act as anchors for the other band players.

One of the middle-aged performers was quite confident, but on this day was struggling slightly with some playing issues. He was quite an experienced performer and had helped many others in the band over time. So, with this person a gentle touch was needed when suggesting how to fix his mechanical issues. A person like this knows what is right and has mentored other young ones in the band, so you need to be careful not to call out their credibility in front of others.

Strong, young, skilled players lacking discipline: there are always a few of these in a group. These people generally have had good teaching at an early age and have possibly progressed a bit too quickly. Their hands may be fast enough and clear enough to play at a good level, but in the big picture they are not in control. They may lose a bit of focus, feel impatient, and/or fail to play with the accurate timing and musical phrasing that the group requires. I am not as gentle with these players, as they need to be shown how they are playing something and then how to do it better. When you can explain to them that they could easily be better than this, then you can often get some discipline into their playing. They have good hands, but their hands are running the show instead of the head.

As you learn to lead, you discover whom you offer advice quietly, gently, or perhaps off to the side, and who you just stop right there and correct immediately.

If you are taking on a leadership role in a music group, it's important to understand what your true position is within that group. There is a broad difference between leading a "fun group" of musicians or being captain of the pickup game in the men's league after work, compared to a top professional sports team or symphony where people are paid a lot of money. The leader in any group, though, has the responsibility to understand the task, organize, and motivate to get the best out of the group of individuals. The leader must know the strengths of the people in their group and delegate when they can to keep their own focus. The leader should always be able to make a point to the group through example. This is what you feel is the best way forward, so speak to your group and get them onside with you so everyone is pursuing the same goal.

There may be several of these smaller goals along the road as you aim towards the bigger goal. Understanding your individual members' personalities and abilities will let you know how far you can take your group.

Most important to note is that everyone, collectively, understands the end goal that the group is after and agrees with the plan. This allows the leader and those on the "leadership team" to help coach, train, teach, remind, urge, or convince the others that working fully as a unit, under the guidance of a selected leader, to obtain a specific goal can result in them delivering their own true awesome performance. When the players work for the leader, and the leader works for the players, you have a benchmark in performance that allows you to quickly evaluate and compare to your group's big picture goals. Then, as the leader, it becomes your job to organize the plan to coach the group by showing again how any part of it could be better, be it through better organization, better focus, or more dedication. This will improve confidence, resulting in better delivery. This can also be another opportunity to use the One-eighty Factor to see how any negative thought, action, or situation can be anticipated and addressed.

Learning to lead is an important skill, not least of all because it helps you to reflect on your effort and your own performance. Sometimes leading others gives *you* a wake-up call on your own shortcomings or areas in need of improvement. In the end, you are also the leader of yourself, so if you wish to become more proficient at your craft, you must apply all of the leadership skills to your own self, to improve yourself and personal performance in any activity you take on.

❖ DALI LAMA OR TONY SOPRANO—IS YOUR LEADING STYLE FULL OF GUIDANCE OR ARE YOU BOSSY?

❖ BE IN CONTROL. ONCE YOU CAN LEAD YOURSELF, THEN YOU CAN LEAD OTHERS.

- What are your own reminders from this chapter?

....

....

....

....

....

....

....

....

....

....

....

....

....

....

....

....

....

....

....

For more information visit www.brucegandymusic.com

SECTION 3
Avoid Mediocrity

How you do anything is how you do everything.
—*T. Harv Eker* (Secrets of the Millionaire Mind)

If you are going to "Deliver Your Own Awesome," accepting mediocrity is not going to get you there.

- You need a compelling life purpose.
- Focus on growing and being the very best you can be.
- Become committed to goals, start them, and *do them every day*.

Don't assume each choice we make affects only the current circumstance. Example: Missing a workout, procrastinating on a project, or eating junk food is "no big deal" as you'll get a "do over" tomorrow. This is where the discipline begins to fail you. Allowing yourself to dismiss the plan you set out will start to limit the level at which you will eventually perform.

Discipline creates lifestyle and that starts with an alarm clock in the morning. Pressing snooze until the last moment will then have you rushing through your day. You will not have the proper time to pursue your dreams and projects and will end up trying to just get by. What you are doing is far more important to who you are becoming.

- Choosing the easy way over the right way shapes you. Sometimes, you must choose the more difficult way, which can help to build the discipline needed for creating great results in life.
- Accountability means the act of being responsible to someone else for some action or result. Once we get to break away from the rules of the house it's easy to lose sight of accountability. We create all sorts of justifications for our actions, which then sends us into *a downward spiral into mediocrity*. When you see or hear this

happening, you need to initiate new systems of accountability and responsibility to get yourself into a place where you can perform your best.

- To help with mediocrity, get an accountable partner. Then on the days you don't feel like
- that workout, or practicing, your partner helps you to feel obligated to do the work.
- *If you live, work, and socialize with a group of people without big goals, you will most likely end up there yourself.* If your goals are big, try to spend time with people with equally big goals. Or learn to gently help your own group of friends to raise their personal goals and maintain a higher level of excellence.

This reflects in pretty much all walks of life.

One of the important commitments you can make is to seek out people who support what you do and increase your circle of influence as well as help get you where you want to go in life. Actively seek them out or meet up with similar folks within your scope of performance.

KEY TAKEAWAYS

❖ BE FULLY DISCIPLINED AND COMMIT TO YOUR GOALS.

❖ DON'T JUST PLAY AIMLESSLY. HAVE YOU STARTED YOUR LIST OF GOALS AND COMMITTED TO THEM, AND ARE YOU WORKING ON THEM DAILY?

❖ PERSONAL SATISFACTION. IS "OK" GOOD ENOUGH? ASK YOURSELF.

❖ THE RIGHT INSPIRATION. SPEND TIME WITH LIKE-MINDED PEOPLE WHO HAVE EQUALING BIG GOALS.

❖ TEST YOUR OWN SELF. DO YOU HAVE AN ACCOUNTABILITY PARTNER?

Your Personal Notes and Experiences

- What are your own reminders from this chapter?

....

....

....

....

....

....

....

....

....

....

....

....

....

....

....

....

....

....

For more information visit www.brucegandymusic.com

SECTION 4
Inspire Others

To *inspire,* in your performance, as described in the Cambridge English dictionary, is "to make someone feel that they want to do something and can do it."

As a performer, whether on stage, out on the course, or on the competition platform, you go through the cycle of practice, rehearsal, and performance. It has taken me many years to realize that after all of the work and preparation, the performance is no longer about you. You may get a personal return of some sort, but the actual performance comes to life when you stop worrying about performing well and instead think about your listeners and how you deliver this performance.

You can leave a listener with a few different feelings while performing. If you are spending your time trying to be absolutely technically perfect and manage to do so, then of course that is one form of success, and many of the listeners will be envious of the ability.

But if you are rehearsed well enough that the mechanical aspects are second nature, you then have the ability to be inside the music itself and you can pour your heart and soul into the delivery. When this happens, the listener becomes truly inspired by the playing.

I recently had a judging assignment with twelve people performing classical pieces. The first and second place were quite easy, as they did a very good job presenting the music and technical aspects on pleasant sounding instruments. But trying to decide third, fourth, and fifth place was initially very difficult.

For a while I found myself adding up the faults of others and trying to add up mistakes to narrow things down easier, but that did not work! Fast forward five or ten minutes and I began to think in my head, "They all had faults, so if I forgive that, who was the most pleasant to listen to?" Instead of being a scorekeeper, I became the listener again, thinking about who inspired me with their effort and their music.

It took me less than two minutes to come to a result by thinking about all of the good. I know that all three of these players did not really get to hear many, if any, of the others perform, so their baseline reference was their own playing, which, due to some errors, they may have all thought was awful. I made a point to find all three competitors to explain to them how I came to my conclusion.

Needless to say, they were happy to get a result, but more so, two of them came back to me later on (one in email) to thank me for the positive spin on their performance. I gave them some ideas on how they might be able to work on the troubled spots instead of just pointing out that I knew they did something incorrectly. These players said to me that this sort of positive feedback was inspiring to them and they were eager to get back at the rehearsal with the new knowledge and possible solutions. Instead of just saying, "You're right there but . . ." or the old, "You got this," I put myself in their shoes and tried to find a way to spin it positively while making sure they understood what needed to be done. Inspiring those players inspires me to want to be better as a person.

When I coach fellow musicians, I try to divide teaching into categories. Some part of the session is devoted to mechanics, whether it is tonal quality of the instrument or working on the technical embellishments. The other half is about the delivery of the music. We must try to motivate and inspire the student when we can on both ends of the session.

People are very good at identifying items or parts which are incorrect or wrong. Yes, it means you are paying attention in some form, but not as a whole. One saying that I try to live by is, *"Don't let the stuff that is incorrect, wrong, or distracting get in the way of the parts which are good."* Pay attention to the whole piece. Even if there is an issue with one of the embellishments, don't cut yourself or student down too hard. If you focus on the part of it that is okay in that movement, or just in front or after it musically, it can be much easier to bring the rest into line with the good parts. The technical movement often gets better more quickly this way instead of just focusing on what's "wrong."

People hear what is wrong with a performance and then at times dwell on it, but this takes away from the listening itself. If you tell a person that you heard them perform and this part and that part were not as good as usual, well, that is not very inspiring. As a coach, you need to inspire people as much as you can, to keep them moving forward in a positive and eager way.

Part of this job is to help a person become inspired by themselves. While I am not a person that writes down all of their goals on paper for everything, I do get some students to break down their goals into small, smaller, and even micro-goals, if we need to. Under the heading of *"Small Steps, but Aim Big,"* a performer must realize that a new piece just doesn't come to life in a day. But it can be hard to see any change or improvement at times.

One method that has worked is the use of audio or video recording. I have asked students to record themselves once or twice a week if need be and date them but do not listen right away, and just carry on for a couple of weeks or even months (depending on their ability and progress). After a while, when the student maybe feels they have hit a plateau or feels like they are not improving at all, I then suggest that we go back and listen to three of those recordings as an exercise. Perhaps one from the middle of their recorded timeline, the most recent recording and one of the earliest recordings. Then, I ask the student to now become the teacher. I instruct them to make a few notes of their own on their paper and then explain to me a few things:

- Tell me first what was good about all three performances (remembering that you are now talking as if you were coaching player A).
- Tell me the areas that need work and how we might go about altering the playing of these certain parts of the score, without upsetting another area of the piece. Example- fixing technical work and losing musical flow.

- Which version of the three recorded pieces was the most enjoyable to listen to and perform?
- Are you seeing and hearing the progress made between the three separate recordings?

When the student hears, with their own ears, the change in performances over time, they usually begin to notice the small gains and become eager to move forward and make it even better. Instead of a coach giving the only feedback, the student has heard a comparative benchmark of their own self playing. They can hear the positive changes that have occurred over the month. They feel inspired to make this even more refined, now that they know they can do it. The student is inspired to be a better performer due to the example you set for them during the coaching sessions.

When hard work meets progress, and those two bump right into success, the personal reward as a coach is unbeatable and the full circle is now complete.

Bruce with long-time student, Andrea Boyd, after her Silver Medal victory 2008.
Photo Credit Anne Spalding

KEY TAKEAWAYS

❖ HELPING OTHERS. ARE YOU INSPIRING OTHERS OR JUST PLEASING YOURSELF WITH COMMENTS?

❖ ALWAYS GIVE ENCOURAGEMENT. INSPIRE OTHERS WITH A POSITIVE SPIN ON THEIR MOVEMENTS/STYLE/PERFORMANCE.

Your Personal Notes and Experiences

- What are your own reminders from this chapter?

....
....
....
....
....
....
....
....
....
....
....
....
....
....
....
....
....
....

For more information visit www.brucegandymusic.*com*

Create your own reminders.

THANKS TO THESE
Special People

Without the help of a tremendous group of friends giving helpful advice and encouragement, this book would have never made it to the shelves (or laptop) for your enjoyment. From the beginning, I had help from people who pushed me through the tougher writing times, corrected statements and generally encouraged the project along. It would like to mention a few people here in particular. At the very beginning, Martha gave me great insight into the whole process of writing itself. Being an author, she was both encouraging and constructive. My great long-time friend Michael Grey gave terrific feedback and helped me with actually starting to lay the pages out into a form that "could" look like a book. Being very visual this was of great assistance to me.

Finally, I can easily say that had it not been for my good friend, the late J David Hester, with his boundless energy, very direct thoughts on how things should be, forcing me to either accept or deny and endlessly pushing me, this book would not be done. I owe a great deal to David for his help and insights as well as convincing me that there really was an end to this project. Many late nights rereading his notes on what I had sent him were always encouraging.

Without all of these people I would have never finished this project. Thank you to all of you!

J David Hester
Jacquie Troy Carter
Martha Moore Davis
Michael Grey
Laura Neville
William Livingstone
Heather Scott Wiseheart
Kathleen Zinck
Zack Arbios
Peter Aumonier

www.ingramcontent.com/pod-product-compliance
Lightning Source LLC
Chambersburg PA
CBHW052344100525
26363CB00003B/9